,106

The Accidental Warden

The Accidental Warden

◆

My unexpected year as Warden of the California Women's Prison

Brook Carey

Best Wishes to Marjorie Brody
Brook Carey 4/28/14

iUniverse, Inc.
New York Bloomington Shanghai

The Accidental Warden
My unexpected year as Warden of the California Women's Prison

Copyright © 2008 by Brook Carey

All rights reserved. No part of this book may be used or reproduced by any means, graphic, electronic, or mechanical, including photocopying, recording, taping or by any information storage retrieval system without the written permission of the publisher except in the case of brief quotations embodied in critical articles and reviews.

iUniverse books may be ordered through booksellers or by contacting:

iUniverse
1663 Liberty Drive
Bloomington, IN 47403
www.iuniverse.com
1-800-Authors (1-800-288-4677)

Because of the dynamic nature of the Internet, any Web addresses or links contained in this book may have changed since publication and may no longer be valid.

ISBN: 978-0-595-48166-8 (pbk)
ISBN: 978-0-595-71967-9 (cloth)
ISBN: 978-0-595-60260-5 (ebk)

Printed in the United States of America

The views expressed in this work are solely those of the author and do not necessarily reflect the views of the publisher, and the publisher hereby disclaims any responsibility for them.

To avoid legal liability, the names of many of those connected with the prison and its administration are altered to conceal identity; ethnicity and gender are retained and the incidents are factual. Because information relating to Charles Manson and the presence of the Manson "girls" at the California Institution for Women is in the public domain, their names are not fictionalized. In the book, the sentences in italics and passages contained within quotations represent the style and tenor of the text.

"If a man will begin in certainties he shall end in doubts; but if he will be content to begin in doubts he shall end in certainties."

—Philosopher Francis Bacon

Contents

The Beginning 1
Some Background 4
Introduction to CIW 6
The Interview 8
The Tour of CIW 12
On the Job 17
March Wardens' Meeting 20
Lunch with the Governor 22
Orientation and Training 25
The Business Office 27
Security and Custody 31
Disciplinary Lockup 38
Counseling and Social Services 40
The Manson "Girls" 43
Food Service 46
Education 48
Regular Hospital 51
Activities 55
Vocational Programs 60

Outside Groups	64
Parole Board	65
Conjugal Visits	67
The CIW Routine	69
Relating with Residents	75
Male/Female Relationships	86
June Wardens' Meeting	89
Manson Family Threat	90
Challenges to be Managed	97
Meeting Charles Manson	101
Warnings of Trouble	105
The Riot	108
Investigation and Resignation	115
In Retrospect	119
Epilogue	122

Thank You

My husband, Bill Carey, is a remarkable Renaissance man. Thank you, Bill, for supporting my year as the Warden at the expense of your own career. I appreciate you for encouraging me to tell my story and your excellent suggestions and valued additions to this account. Thank you for being my special, valued soul mate.

Acknowledgement

My friend, Marie Ferrante, is an exceptional graphic designer. Her preliminary drawing was the inspiration of the front cover design. Visit her work on-line http://www.marieferrante.com/. Thank you, Marie, for your generous assistance.

A Special Remembrance

Beverly Morgan was my secretary at the prison. She was outstanding in every way. After I resigned, she became a Correctional Officer at the California Institution for Men. She and her husband, George, visited Bill and me several times over the next few years and kept in touch. We were close friends. Sadly, a malignant brain tumor took this special person when she was still very young. She is greatly missed and never forgotten.

The Beginning

If someone had warned me on March 4, 1975 that I soon would be heading the women's prison in California, experiencing a **dan**gerous prison riot first hand and meeting Charlie Manson to discuss his "girls," I would have said they were crazy.

When I arrived that evening at our Birmingham, Michigan home from my consulting business, I had no idea that my life was about to upend. Things started out normally. Bill, my husband of almost three years was waiting to greet me. *Hi sweetheart, how was your day?*

I hugged him. *Hello my darling, I think I got a new client—that fellow from Chicago who wants to relocate to Detroit. And how were things for you?*

Bill grinned. *We had some visiting brass from Washington that I had to entertain. GM always draws the heat when the politicians want to pressure the auto industry. But it was no problem. I managed to handle it without getting my foot in my mess kit.*

Bill never complained about his job. He was happy to have made a successful transition to an Industry/Government Relations Staff job at General Motors after retiring from the Army as a Lieutenant Colonel. While many of his Army colleagues were also successful in transitioning into the corporate world, many were content to have a second career in sales.

As we sat in the family room enjoying a cocktail and our classical music collection, I could tell something was on Bill's mind. Then impatiently he asked me when I was going to look at the mail. On top of the pile of letters placed on the coffee table was a white envelope bearing the return address: **Corrections Department, Sacramento, California**. It was addressed to me. As I opened it, I remembered.

I remembered that past December sitting in my career counseling office scanning the *Wall Street Journal* classified ads. This was a daily routine in an attempt to find job opportunities for my clients. It was then that I spotted an ad in the Western edition:

Superintendent of Women's Correctional Institution
Position available for experienced Administrator.
No corrections experience needed. Salary: $29,688.

Send résumé to Corrections Department
Human Relations Department, Sacramento, CA

The ad did not specify they were seeking a woman, but I suspected that was the case. What a great opportunity for one of my female clients, I thought. Men will apply, but a woman will be selected. I scouted through my client files and selected three women who appeared to be qualified. I thought they all would be interested. In 1975 there weren't many opportunities in business for women to earn almost $30,000 a year ($48,000 in 2007 dollars.) When I phoned them, each said the salary would be great but then they gave weak excuses as to why they weren't interested. I was disappointed in their collective rejections of a rewarding and challenging opportunity. How can women get ahead if they're not career-minded and willing to take risks?

When I told Bill about it he immediately said *Why don't you apply? You have the right credentials. You'd be great in that job!* With dinner on hold we started to discuss the possibilities of this offer. Our four children were in college or private schools. Bill is a California native and thinks of it as home in spite of twenty-two rootless years in the military. Being a Western man, he never really liked living in the Detroit area. He reassured me saying *Now that we're married I don't care where we live as long as we're together.*

We agreed it would be gratifying for me to hold an important, responsible position while having the opportunity to make a significant difference in a large system. This position would offer me a chance to help some of those unfortunate women who are locked away from their children and families. The following day I assembled my résumé and mailed it off to Sacramento giving it little afterthought until now. The letter was to the point.

Dear Mrs. Carey:

Congratulations. You have been selected from a field of over three hundred top administrators as one of the three finalists in a nationwide search to fill the position of Superintendent (Warden) of the Frontera California Institution for Women (CIW), the only woman's prison in California. It is one of the largest women's prisons in the country and enjoys a world-wide reputation for being in the forefront of correctional programs for women.

We have arranged a panel interview for you and two other finalists on Monday, March 10, 1975. Please call my office as soon as possible to confirm the time and for further details about the requirements of the interview. We look forward to meeting you personally.

Sincerely,

Carlos Sanchez
Director, Human Resources

I knew you could do it, sweetheart! You're the best there is! Bill grinned and hugged me. *Hey, it feels great to hug a Warden!*

But they haven't picked me, yet. And maybe they won't. But what if they do? I don't know anything about running a prison. And what about General Motors? Nobody ever quits GM!

Don't worry, Bill assured me. *GM can survive without Bill Carey on their payroll. Anyway, we can deal with the details later. I'll take a couple of vacation days and fly out with you. We'll rent a car at the airport and visit my mother in Palm Springs over the weekend. It'll be fun. Then I'll drive you to the prison Monday morning. I can hang out at the Library in Chino while you have the interview.*

So without any more serious consideration than that, it was decided. And our lives were about to undergo extensive, enduring changes.

Some Background

I was forty-four when I started working at the California Institute for Women. Up to that time, my life and career were varied and unpredictable. I divorced my first husband when I was twenty-eight and was a single mother for almost thirteen years. I met and married Bill Carey in 1972 at forty-one; he was a widower at forty-three. We each had two adult children. In 1975 we still were like newlyweds. Although I married Bill because he was the smartest man I had ever met, his handsome face and tall muscular body were added attractions. His twenty-two years in the military, including Intelligence and Green Beret training, had toughened him physically and mentally. He liked to tease me *How do you like being married to a trained killer?* But he was more of a lover than a fighter; fiercely protective of me, and tender at the right times. I adored him.

I began my career in 1961 as a secretary, after dropping out of college the first year. I perfected my office skills and advanced in several companies, always becoming the "top female" in the company (but never earning more than a modest wage.) In my last job in 1971, I was Assistant to the President of an auto parts die casting company. When plated plastic replaced plated die castings the company went out of business. At that point I'd had enough of being an employee, so I established my own consulting company, Executeam, specializing in professional office management. I hired two consultant trainees, and we became what I believe was the first all-female business consulting firm in the country.

My consulting business was very successful, so I then expanded into career counseling and résumé writing. A year later I established an employment agency and a management search firm. My friends called me a "mini-conglomerate." I loved having all those "plates in the air."

My lack of formal college education was a personal embarrassment. For many years I read textbooks, not novels, and educated myself in a variety of business subjects. In 1974, I decided to work toward a Master of Business Administration degree and approached the University of Detroit Graduate School of Business. *You can't be admitted here without an Undergraduate degree* they said. Full of confidence, I replied *I'm sorry, but I don't believe you. I believe you will want to admit me to your Graduate program. I would like to speak to someone else, please.* I knew they would not pick me up bodily and throw me out the door nor would they call the campus security guard so I held my ground. What did I have to lose? They already had said *NO*.

I was referred up the chain of command through three more negative staffers until I reached the Dean of the Graduate School himself. He was a grizzled former Navy Commander who eyed me curiously. *Come with me, young lady. We're going to lunch!* He drove me downtown to the London Chop House, one of the finer restaurants in Detroit where we enjoyed a three hour lunch. When he learned that I was running six businesses he decided that I might make an interesting addition to the MBA class. It was decided to admit me if I could pass the graduate school entrance exam and maintain a B average. I did both and began industriously working on my degree.

The second semester, I had to take an **Advanced Statistics** course. The first day of class I realized that I couldn't pass that course, not having had **Introduction to Statistics** or any advanced mathematics courses. So that's when I knew that my dream of earning an MBA was never to be. My academic credentials then stated that I was working toward an MBA degree, not that I had earned it. Apparently that was enough for the California Department of Corrections to decide that I was more than qualified.

I did not give enough thought to the question "what if I am selected for the prison warden position?" My self-confidence has always been high and I labored under the premise that I could do virtually anything. I had never worked up to my full potential and therefore some of my confidence was based on probability rather than past accomplishments. As I prepared to go to California for the interview, I had no expectation of being selected. I just thought the interview and learning about the prison system would be a valuable experience. Well, it was a valuable experience, but not in the way I had anticipated.

Introduction to CIW

Monday, March 10, 1975, 8:00 A.M. The weekend visit with Bill's mother in Palm Springs was a welcome respite but I was eager to have the interview. The Southern California way of life and natural beauty were indeed several thousand miles removed from Michigan. We had left chilly, rainy Detroit and arrived in the sunny desert that was just beginning to bloom with verbena and Indian paint brush. Mexican poppies and lupine softened the stance of the prickly cholla cactus. The pastel-colored Southern California houses sporting bright tile roofs were curiosities to my conservative Midwestern taste. California is many things to many people and I am one of the many people that indeed found many reasons to become a westerner.

Bill and I left Palm Springs early to drive to CIW that was located east of Chino in the midst of numerous dairy farms. It was hard to believe that some thirty miles west of Chino was the sprawling metropolis of Los Angeles. The rosy dawn revealed the craggy peaks of San Gorgonio and San Jacinto as we sped west. I wanted to arrive in time to take the tour of the prison that Carlos had suggested. Bill felt at home in the desert where he was raised. Driving along, he pointed out many places and things, relishing being my teacher.

The letter I received had "Frontera" California as the address, but Frontera was not on the map. It is a fictitious location that accommodates only CIW, the women's prison. Frontera is the Spanish word for frontier. Its name conceals that it is a prison. When inmates' families write to an inmate, the only address necessary is the inmate's name and Frontera, California.

As we neared CIW, the landscape changed to dairy farm lands, for miles and miles. It was flat, green, with occasional muddy pens where thousands of dairy cows milled and mooed. The smell of manure was strong so we drove along with the windows tightly closed. The double lane road took many turns, seeming to go nowhere. Then, suddenly, looming in the middle of the cow pastures was a giant smokestack. Nearby were many single-story red-brick buildings, set back from the road, surrounded by a tall chain-link fence topped with simple barbed wire. There were no guard towers at the corners of the perimeter fence but merely small guard booths that looked like outhouses and appeared to be empty. In my mind I had envisioned a stone fortress with massive walls scaling thirty feet into the sky. This sprawling facility resembling a community college campus was the last thing I had expected to encounter. I learned later the campus-like design was a result of the 1950s progressive notion of offenders' rehabilitation.

The parking lot next to the U-shaped driveway was filled with cars. Bill pulled up in front of the central building. The sign read **Administration.** He leaned over and kissed me. *Call me at the Library in Chino when you're ready. I'll be in the reading room. I'll scout out a place for dinner before we catch our plane back to Detroit.*

My moment was at hand.

The Interview

I walked briskly into the Administration Building. The lobby area looked like a registration desk in a cheap motel with a Formica counter on the right and a group of shabby plastic chairs on the left. Directly in front of this reception area was a security barrier consisting of a counter with glass extending to the ceiling. This barrier contained a door that opened with a buzzer, topped by a glass window. Beyond this control point was a hallway leading to a second area that resembled a waiting room in a small-town bus station. This obviously was the inmates' Visiting Room. There were no bars, only glass barriers. I paused to study the Mission Statement on the wall.

> *The primary mission of the California Institution for Women is to provide a safe and secure environment for female offenders. This mission is further defined by our responsibility to provide quality health care and Institutional programs specifically geared to meet the special needs of female offenders.*

I thought that was a mission I could support.

I approached the uniformed man at the reception counter. *I'm Brook Carey. I'm expected for an interview for the Warden position. They told me to ask for Florence.* At that moment, a tall, slim man standing next to me at the counter turned with a smile. He looked like a high caliber traveling salesman who was checking into a motel. He appeared to be in his mid forties, good-looking, vigorous, with gray-hair.

"*So, you're Brook Carey. How do you do? I'm John Dietler. And just between us at CIW the position is referred to as <u>Superintendent</u>, not Warden.* He smiled again. I felt confused because his name was unfamiliar. I did not know who he was, if he was there to interview me, or how he fitted in. Apparently my résumé had preceded me. I smiled and shook hands.

(I learned later that John was employed by the Corrections Department in its Prison Industry Authority, as the liaison with industry. His job was to bring lay people from various industries to the prisons to create jobs and to provide vocational training and jobs for inmates. Visiting CIW on his regular schedule, I found him to be a pleasant introduction to this strange new world. John was the only person I knew in the Corrections Department who came from the business world. We immediately liked each other and became good friends. He was my biggest fan in the Corrections Department—he thought I was a perfect person to bring a new perspective to the operations of this prison. He seemed to find reasons to visit CIW and be supportive of me. He seemed to sense when I needed someone to give advice. He was my mentor—the one person I met in the system who spoke my language, understood me and could relate. We were two of a kind.)

Before I had a chance to react to John Dietler, the reception officer beckoned me through a door that "buzzed" open and pointed me down a long hall. The interior of the Administration Building reconfirmed my first impression. It looked like a community college building—linoleum flooring, the kind that scoops up the sides of the walls for more efficient mopping. I assumed the portraits on the walls were of people who were significant in the history of the place.

Feeling disoriented, I entered the Superintendent's secretary's office, a bare institutional-looking room, with a few drooping potted plants on the window sill. An attractive woman, dressed in an expensive-looking suit, stepped forward, introducing herself as Florence.

Hello, Florence, I came early. They told me to ask for you, to arrange a tour.

Yes, she said. *I'll be happy to do that. You just have a seat.* She hurried away, returning in a few minutes. *They're still interviewing one of the other candidates, so we have time for a quick tour. Come along* she said briskly.

Just then the door to the Superintendent's office opened and an impressive-looking woman (I guessed this was a job candidate) exited. I could see three people sitting around a table in the room. So my tour was postponed. I stepped into the room and was introduced to the "panel" from the Corrections Department: Walt Cooper (Director of Prisons), Carrie Johnson (Director Affirmative Action) and Carlos Sanchez (Director Human Resources.) This panel was known collectively to the CIW employees as the "brass." Walt Cooper was good-looking with dark hair and eyes and a good build. Carlos Sanchez looked Hispanic, which he was. He was thin, medium build and had narrow eyes. He had a friendly smile. Carrie Johnson was an attractive African American with reddish and carefully coiffed hair.

I had tried to prepare for this interview by reading library books about women's prisons. There were only a few books on this subject available in 1975. One of the most interesting, *Making it in Prison: the Square, the Cool and the Life*, by Esther Heffernan, Publisher: New York, Wiley-Interscience [1972], was about a prison in the East. It portrayed career criminals, women whom the staff could not influence or help. That book and others painted the worst pictures of the challenges and the hopelessness of the women's prison systems. I knew virtually nothing about the criminal justice system, none of the problems, none of the jargon. I did not know it was a political game. However, being a professional interviewer and career developer, I did know about interviews. The panel's small talk put me somewhat at ease so I decided to take charge of this interview by taking a short-cut.

My résumé tells you what I know how to do. Perhaps it will better serve our time constraints if I tell you who I am. The three exchanged mildly surprised glances but motioned me to continue. *I believe I'm an effective manager and administrator. I'm interested in helping people. My motivation is much different than the average person's.* They asked questions and I replied as honestly and as originally as I could. *You should know that I relate well with people but probably care too much about their problems. I don't have a high level of personal defenses. I'm a humanist, not a tough person. I'm brave but I'm not suited to play a hard-hitting role.*

They asked my motives for wanting to be Superintendent. I thought I had managed the interview up to now. But I was feeling a little disoriented and at that point, I did not care if they selected me. So I blurted out the core of my self-interest. *My main motive is … the real reason is … well, what if? … what if a woman who is self-actualized, who doesn't have an axe to grind, who isn't neurotic or screwed up, who is emotionally mature, who doesn't need the money. What if that woman would be in charge of one of the largest women's prisons in the country? What could she to accomplish? What could she improve? What if a woman who did that wasn't doing it for herself? I believe I am the woman who can do this, who can make a significant contribution to this place, who can improve things. And I think this situation normally doesn't attract people with my type of business and administrative background.*

This aside for readers of this book is my personal philosophy of behavior, inserted here to help readers better understand me and my motivations.

For most of my life I had endeavored to be "perfect" to earn my parents' approval but never quite succeeded. This problem affects many people in our culture. I believe this is the result of the passage in the **King James Bible** where Jesus tells his disciples to be "perfect." Interestingly, when the Dead Sea Scrolls were discovered, one of the Scrolls *contained that very* **Bible** *passage. And translation of the word "perfect" revealed that the word meant "whole" or "unbroken" as in the "perfect chalice." When I learned of this in my thirties, I changed my aspiration from trying to be a "perfect" person to working toward being a "whole" person. I created for myself a definition of a whole person as exhibiting three important qualities. A whole person*

1. *gives generously and spontaneously to others. (As children, we are taught to be generous, but giving spontaneously requires practice.)*

2. *receives graciously. (This helps others to give and be "whole.")*

3. *never is a "taker." (Never takes credit unduly, never demands love, never is selfish.)*

A whole person doesn't worry about failure or making a mistake. If I never failed or made a mistake, I wouldn't be involved in the world. A whole person makes decisions knowing that the moment of absolute certainty will never arrive.

I taught this philosophy to my children and practiced it every day, myself. This simple action made me a much improved person with a happier family.

The panel members exchanged approving glances. Walt Cooper nodded. *I agree with you, Mrs. Carey. We want to try a new approach, and we want someone from outside Corrections, a strong administrator. It appears that you have the background to run a tight ship with the limited budget you will have to work with. Do you have any questions, Mrs. Carey?* It seemed the interview was concluding. I said *If you do select me, I'm sure I'll have many questions later. Is there anything more you'd like to tell me now?*

No, but after Florence takes you on a tour of the campus, please return to the secretary's office. I was puzzled that we hadn't talked about the inmates and their problems and prospects for rehabilitation. No, this had been more like being interviewed to be the Office Manager. Thinking back, I should have seen more clues about what was to come. But I was feeling more comfortable, eager to get my first glimpse of the inside of a woman's prison.

The Tour of CIW

As I emerged into the secretary's office, a slim, brown-skinned woman, who I assumed was the third candidate, was invited into the interview room. I later learned that she was from the East, had a Ph.D. in Sociology and was my nearest competitor.

A visibly excited Florence led me back down the hall of the Administration Building. *Oh, Mrs. Carey, I've heard so much about you. Your résumé portrays such an interesting background. It's my great pleasure to take you on a tour of the campus. About the campus? That's what we call the central yard. And we don't call the women here convicts or inmates. We call them <u>residents</u>.*

Turning right, we were buzzed through the door into the Residents' Visiting Room. Next to it, visible through a glass wall, was the Control Center, the heart of the custody system. The Control Center was a room with dimmed lighting and electronic control panels on three sides like the control tower at the airport. There were three or four uniformed people watching silently over the controls. As we paused by the door leading from the Visiting Room to the campus, a Correctional Officer nodded through the glass and buzzed us through.

Close up, the one-story buildings ringing the center walkways looked even more like a community college. In the center was a broad expanse of a green-lawn commons-area, with paved walks crossing in several directions. Park benches were placed under the trees and I saw dozens of residents going about their business, walking, sitting and lounging on the grass. The residents were dressed in street clothes, not prison uniforms. Most wore jeans or shorts and T-shirts. Many displayed elaborate hair styles and make-up. No one was shuffling along in thongs, as I had expected. All my stereotypes from "women in the cage" movies evaporated.

No one had told me about my personal safety, walking in the campus. I did not know if some resident would leap out at me with a knife, or make a life threatening move toward me. *Is it safe for me to be out here on the campus, Florence?*

She chuckled. *It's pretty safe. Anyway, you're with me.* With her manicured nails and high-style hairdo, Florence did not look like a person who could provide security for anyone, but she was so blithe about it that I decided to show a brave face. She was most interested in showing me the bricks and mortar of the place. She chattered along about the buildings we passed, ignoring the residents. Obviously she knew the ropes.

This is the Education Building. We entered a low building that resembled an elementary school—little library, little audio-visual room, little classrooms. I expected to see bulletin boards with the alphabet on them.

Let me show you our vocational rooms. This is the LVN room. Residents can study to be Licensed Vocational Nurses. Some of these students train in the hospital in town.

I was startled. *Isn't that a great risk? What if they try to escape?*

But Florence was bustling down the hall. She proudly said *Cosmetology uses these rooms. See, we have shampoo bowls, hair dryers and stylists stations, everything, just like the outside.*

I cleared my throat. *Do the inmates, I mean the residents, use regular scissors and razors in here?* I was feeling uneasy.

Of course, she said, looking amused. *How else could they cut hair?*

We glanced into the Arts and Crafts room featuring a pottery wheel and kiln. *It must be good therapy for the residents, to have a creative outlet. I've read that arts and crafts play an important part in rehabilitation.* Florence regarded me quizzically and replied *I suppose so, but this kiln hasn't worked in months. There's no money to fix it. And there's no money for craft items. The residents used to make craft items to sell in the Visiting Room. That way, the residents could earn money for their prison bank accounts established in their names. Unfortunately, the Art teacher quit in disgust when the program money ran out.*

As we were continuing our tour I suddenly smelled something burning—an acrid type odor. Someone has set the building on fire, I thought. I am a leader, I have to respond. But this was a strange place where I had no road map and could be in physical danger from the residents. In spite of that, as an action person, I felt responsible to take charge to do something like alert Security to isolate this potential threat.

Florence, have you had any emergency or resident restraint training since you've worked here? I needed to understand the procedures that should be followed in any emergency.

She turned to me, astonished. *I'm the Superintendent's assistant secretary but I'm not staff. I'm a resident here. Didn't you know that?* So here I was, the legal authority dealing with an emergency while under guidance of a resident. And here was the resident, Florence, who wasn't at all concerned about it.

There was a classroom at the end of the hall, near the acrid odor, so I knocked at the door and entered. The dozen or so women sitting on student desks around in a circle looked up in surprise. Because they were dressed in street clothes, I did not know who the residents were, and who the staff members were. Maybe none were staff members!

I think there may be a fire I said in what I hoped was a firm voice. One woman looked up without moving. A teacher, I hoped. *I'll check it out* she said languidly. Confused thoughts tumbled through my mind. Are they testing me to take charge or are they "doing a job" on me? Is this some kind of escape plan? Am I over-reacting? No one seemed to be worried about the odor. Am I just being naïve? The residents were exchanging knowing looks with Florence. Only later I learned that the odor was marijuana and the residents were enjoying an illegal smoke. Luckily, before I did anything foolish, the loudspeaker sputtered and squawked outside.

BROOK CAREY, PLEASE REPORT TO ADMINISTRATION

Florence and I hurried back to the Administration Building, through the buzzer doors and down the hall. The panel members were waiting for me in the secretary's office. *Congratulations, Superintendent! Yes, we've selected you. Welcome aboard, Mrs. Carey, er Brook. This starts a challenging new career for you. We'll get word to the press right away.*

I was in such shock that I did not even think it was strange when Florence rushed forward and gave me a hearty hug. They kept congratulating me as if they had just finished an unpleasant chore. I tried to sort it all out. I needed to think, to talk to Bill about this. What were the terms of the job offer? Was this really a valid job offer? My thoughts were whirling.

Brook, we want you to stay here in California to take charge immediately. We want you to go to Claremont, near Los Angeles the day after tomorrow to attend the Wardens' quarterly meeting and be introduced. Tell your husband that you're on the payroll effective tomorrow and you should send him home to pack. We have to leave for the Chino airport now to fly back to Sacramento. We'd like you to ride along to the airport with us so we can discuss final details on the way. OK?

This was moving too fast for me. I said firmly *But my husband is picking me up here in a half-hour. He's at the Library in Chino in the reading room.* So Florence phoned Bill at the Library and told him to head for the Chino airport. I jumped into the car with the "brass" and sped to the small airport. They all seemed to be talking at once, but nothing was said about the ground rules, the salary, the benefits and what was expected of me. I still was in shock over being hired. Why hadn't I done more homework? I should have talked more to Bill about the implications. He'd said, if you get the job, I'll quit mine and we'll move to California. That was how we superficially had considered it. We owned a house, a corporation and several going businesses. We had our friends and my parents to consider. What job would Bill hold in California? Serious things we hadn't discussed because I believed that if I was selected it would be by accident. Now, here I was—the accidental Warden.

The car careened down the dusty road through the cow pastures and squealed through the gate of the small airport stopping abruptly. The "brass" hurried toward the small, private plane purring on the runway. Someone called *Hey, don't worry, it'll all work out. We'll call you at CIW tomorrow*. With a wave in my direction, they quickly boarded the plane that taxied and roared away. So there I was—no preparation, no chance to go home and think about it and not enough clothes or personal necessities to last a weekend. My mind was numb. Turning from the runway, I saw Bill in our rental car rushing toward me. He parked and came running. His strong arms around me felt like the first reality of the past few hours.

What's going on?
I was hired!
Well, what's the deal?
I don't know. But I'm on the job, starting tomorrow.
Oh, my God!
Yeah.

"Yeah" was a grand understatement! Not only was my business career turned upside down but my life with Bill was about to undergo an unexpected separation, with mutual comfort and advice available only by daily phone calls. Matters were made worse with Bill heading back to Michigan by himself with multiple challenges of leaving General Motors, closing my businesses, selling our house and moving our possessions to Southern California.

After dinner that evening, with a lot of hand-holding Bill deposited me at the Pine Tree Motel, a modest lodging in Chino, characterized by a gigantic pine tree in front. With a lingering embrace, he was off to the Ontario Airport for a night flight back to Detroit. The motel would be my residence until I could find a permanent place to call home. My motel room had no telephone and was sparsely furnished. Communication with CIW was through the night clerk at the front desk.

The CIW Superintendent was no longer provided living quarters on the prison grounds. Those quarters above the Superintendent's office had been converted to Family Visiting Units for the residents. Thinking about that, I was pleased to have a retreat at the motel away from the prison. As I unpacked my small suitcase I was concerned that I had brought only enough clothes for a three day stay. I knew Bill would select the essentials from my closet back in Michigan to send them me. The staff members had mentioned that whatever outfit the Superintendent wears to the office is fodder for gossip and speculation among the residents.

In spite of these challenging conditions, we still had a couple of arrows in our shared quiver. Bill's military life style had equipped him to pull up roots, sever ties and move on in an orderly and thorough manner. My forte was never to avoid a challenge or opportunity and always attempt to do my best work even in uncharted waters. It all came together in a matter of several months. Bill completed his check list and I found time away from CIW to purchase our new "nest in the west" in Riverside, some fifteen miles from the prison. This was all done with only one trip back to Detroit for me and no dry runs to California for Bill until he pulled into our driveway the following May. Thereafter, my learning curve at CIW was further enhanced by dinner table and "pillow talk"—much preferred to a voice on the phone.

On the Job

Tuesday, March 11, 1975, 8:00 A.M. It was time to report to work. I was assigned the "Superintendent's car." It was a high mileage American Motors compact car used by staff members to transport residents during weekdays. It was mine to use after hours and on weekends if required for official business.

Turning into the circular drive in front of the CIW Administration Building, I saw a large sign in front of the building written in English and Spanish warning: **It Is a Felony to Bring Contraband Into The Institution. By Order of The Superintendent, Mrs. Brook Carey.** Contraband included liquor, drugs, firearms and potentially dangerous hand held objects. The sign was somewhat faded but my name was newly painted. It was a shock to see my name there. I prefer "Ms." and never use "Mrs." But the staff members were proud to have a woman again as Superintendent, and "Brook" did not convey "female."

In the lobby of the Administration Building was a new sign behind the reception officer's desk reading "Welcome Mrs. Brook Carey—We Need You." Although the reception officer recognized me, I still had to sign in. *We're so glad you're here* he enthused while escorting me around his desk and through the electrically activated door into the hall of the Administration Building. I quickly found the office where I had been interviewed; the door bore new letters: "Office of the Superintendent, Mrs. Brook Carey." No one was in the secretary's office, so I walked through it into my office. On the desk was a large purple chrysanthemum plant with a note, "Welcome to CIW, from Maintenance." I later learned that the flowers were from the Maintenance Supervisor who managed the CIW greenhouse.

So there I was, all by myself—my first day as Superintendent. Shortly, the Fire Captain, who also was the Locksmith, entered, presenting me with a large ring of keys (looking just like a Western movie jail keys.) *Welcome Mrs. Carey! Here are your keys. I hope everything goes well. So long.* Nothing on the keys indicated what locks they opened. This entire morning, so far, was quite strange.

I investigated my three-room office "suite" which was plain and institutional but adequate. A couch and several upholstered chairs facing a large curved blonde-wood desk were the furnishings for the Superintendent. A short hall from my office led to a private toilet room beyond which was a large conference room with table and chairs for eighteen.

When seated in my desk chair I could see through a plate glass window to my left covering almost the complete wall. I could watch residents crossing the campus and lounging on the grass. This window also afforded a good view of the residents' cottage units. Within these units each resident had a private room (these were not called cells) with a barred window and a solid steel door with a small barred window. Each cottage unit was three wings with three community bathrooms/showers. In the hub of the wings was a Control Room with a Correctional Officer stationed there with telephones and electronic controls that opened and closed the doors to the residents' rooms. In addition there was an office for the Correctional Counselor assigned to that cottage. Nearby to these cottages was a large round mess hall called the Village Cafeteria with three separate dining room wings with a central kitchen serving the three dining areas.

After studying the campus layout from my office I decided to go through the IN BASKET on my disk to see what papers were there and figure out what should be done with them. At this point an attractive middle-aged blonde woman entered, introducing herself as Shirley, my secretary. Shirley informed me that the latest count was 750 residents and 330 employees, about 220 of whom were Correctional Officers. She presented the scheduling calendar and told me of all the meetings I was to attend, which were about five a day. Suddenly my telephone rang. *There's a disturbance in the Hospital* reported a nameless voice. Without any thought, I hurriedly left my office and walked rapidly to the regular care Hospital wing of the Administration Building. Noise of the melee elevated as I neared the intake desk of the Hospital wing. There were muffled shouting and swearing as a number of residents were fighting with each other, and several Correctional Officers were trying to subdue the action.

This fighting is useless, I thought. Whatever the problem is, surely it can be settled verbally. Confident of my verbal skills, I plunged into the middle of the disturbance. Immediately two Correctional Officers rushed after me, grabbed me and pulled me to a corner of the room. They were concerned for my safety. I did not know it then, but the California Corrections Department does not recognize hostage-taking. Therefore, if a staff member is taken hostage, the Corrections Department will not bargain. Inmates knew that, thank God. At least I think they knew that. Lesson learned!

That evening back at the motel, I reviewed my first day on the job: Receiving a ring of keys to unknown locks, becoming involved in a disturbance between a group of residents, attending a couple of unmemorable meetings, reviewing the files of several residents and finally, working down to the bottom of my IN BASKET. Many of these events were shared with Bill in our almost nightly phone calls. These calls really kept us going with the sharing of advice to one another and small talk that helped ease the loneliness. That evening I vowed, over the ensuing weeks, to hone my pro-active skills while learning all I could about the prison and its people. While Bill could cook for himself at home and had friends to socialize with, I knew I had to develop some sort of an evening routine to include frequenting local restaurants and participating in civic activities.

March Wardens' Meeting

Wednesday, March 12, 1975. The thirteen California prison Wardens met quarterly for updates and information exchanges. This day we were seated around a U-shaped table in a large conference room at Griswold's Hotel, Claremont, California. I was the only woman at the table. Walt Cooper, my immediate boss, was in charge of the meeting. It seemed like a typical middle management meeting in which the philosophies of running a prison and specific problems being encountered by certain prisons were discussed. The other Wardens were cordial, reassuring me that everything was going to be all right. They must have sensed my confusion and lack of corrections experience.

Walt Cooper told me Ron Burke, a Program Administrator from the California Institution for Men (CIM) in Chino who had been trained as a Correctional Officer at Folsom Prison, was the Department's choice to be one of the two new Deputy Superintendents at CIW. I assumed there weren't any female candidates available at that time because women weren't trained in the system, few women in the Corrections Department had roles that would lead to prison management.

CIW had a serious custody problem record. I was told that Virginia Carlson, the permanent Superintendent before I was appointed, had almost one hundred escapes by residents climbing over the perimeter fence. Ron Burke was specifically selected because he was a "custody" expert. In the system you're either a "custody" expert or a "treatment" expert, but seldom both. Prisons tend to assume different profiles depending on the inmate populations at the time. They move back and forth from being custody prisons to treatment prisons.

I met Ron Burke at the Warden's meeting. He was a tall, broad-shouldered, lanky fellow with bright blue eyes and a western drawl. He was about twelve years younger than I, and appeared to be both intelligent and committed. He understood how the system operated, was comfortable with the bureaucracy and how to work within it. We seemed to share the same philosophies about working with people. I felt that our chemistry would be complimentary, so I accepted Walt Cooper's selection of him. He was speedily appointed and introduced at the meeting as a new Deputy Superintendent of CIW.

At the end of the Wardens' meeting I was told that Governor Jerry Brown wanted to meet me, as he was appointing me to the position. That was the first I learned that I was being appointed rather then hired. Being appointed would be serving "at the pleasure of the Governor." I was concerned, what if he didn't like me? Walt Cooper brushed aside my fears saying *Don't worry about that, this is just a formality and, by the way, after Jerry Brown approves you, then you will have to be confirmed by the California Senate.* This was all news to me. Meantime, back in Birmingham, Bill was selling our house, and had resigned his job at General Motors effective the end of March. It was too late to change my mind. So I put on my best air of confidence and awaited developments.

Lunch with the Governor

Monday, March 17, 1975. Shortly after I settled into my first days at CIW, I was contacted by Harold Williams, who told me to fly to Oakland for a meeting with the Governor. Harold was the Chief Deputy Director in the Corrections Department reporting to Jiro "Jerry" Enomoto who was the Director. The following Monday, in my most professional suit and white gloves, I boarded the plane. Sitting three abreast next to an attractive woman and her husband, I noticed she was reading Junior League materials. I mentioned that I had done consulting for the Junior League in Michigan and we chatted. I confided that I was going to lunch with Governor Brown and would soon be relocating to Southern California. At this point she began elbowing her husband to get his attention. He turned out to be Tom Walker, a well regarded real estate broker in Riverside, some fifteen miles east of Chino, who was flying up for a real estate meeting. He got the hint and passed over his business card. We did purchase a house near Riverside from him; Tom and his wife became good friends with Bill and me.

I deplaned in Oakland where Governor Brown was attending a Board meeting nearby at the University of California at Berkeley. His chauffeur met me and drove to a seafood restaurant near the campus where we were to rendezvous. The chauffeur and I sat in a large booth. Suddenly there he was, Governor Jerry Brown, striding toward us accompanied by a tall burly man. We shook hands and all sat down. No one introduced the burly fellow. I never did learn his full name or the purpose of his attending lunch with us, so it was an awkward situation. I finally said *My name is Brook Carey, what's yours?* He responded that his name was Frank, but did not say who or what he was. In retrospect I concluded he was a member of the Governor's security detail.

The Governor almost immediately was besieged by a group of students and waiters seeking autographs. He said *Governors are not movie stars, and I don't give autographs. I'm just an ordinary man.* I thought, he also is sending me a signal, so I'll just treat him as an ordinary man. This, of course, was a major blunder!

We ordered lunch. The Governor had a bowl of fish chowder and bread that immediately had his full attention. He did not talk to me, so Frank, the chauffeur and I ate our lunches in silence. The Governor finally turned to me and said abruptly *You've never been a Warden before, what makes you think you'll make a Warden now?* I felt tempted to say *You've never been a Governor before, what makes you think you'll make a Governor?* But that would have been an out-of-line response so I just thought it. I replied *I believe I'm an excellent administrator and quite self-actualized.* Then he asked me a couple of penetrating questions regarding my philosophy about criminals, how did I feel about felons and the death penalty. He asked only a few questions without comments, then turned to Frank and began to speak to him in Latin.

I was astonished. He then reached into his shirt pocket and gave me a small blue plastic strip label with gold printing on it, a Latin phrase, AGE QUOD AGIS. That was his motto, he declared, saying that it meant **whatever you are doing for the moment, do that well.** I was sitting in stunned silence during this. The only Latin I could remember was a cartoon in my high school Latin textbook showing a police officer pulling a speeder over to the side of the road and writing a ticket, saying UBI IGNAS EST? (Where is the fire?) Turning to Frank, the Governor began to talk this time in English about the University and some of its problems. It was interesting conversation so I began to follow it chiming in here and there. This startled the Governor because he was ignoring me but I was regaining my composure and confidence. Mistake Number Two occurred when I assumed the Governor meant it when he said he was "just a person" so I joined the conversation.

I knew little about the political history of California. I had heard of Governor Pat Brown and knew Jerry Brown was his son. Some of the comments he made about the University led me to believe he was an apolitical person, rather than a politically motivated one. But I found him to be an abrupt person. Maybe that comes with his title. He acted as though he did not know how to converse comfortably with women. I felt that he had particular difficulty relating to an independently-minded woman like me. On the other hand, he exuded charisma that almost could be physically felt as he approached our luncheon booth. But in spite of my first impressions of him I respected and admired him. In our brief conversation, he darted in and out, and fixed me with a keen gaze like he was looking right into me. He made no attempt to get to know me but I felt he was probing my brain to decide if I was an intelligent, well-balanced person. It took him two or three minutes to figure that out, and after that it was insignificant.

The Governor abruptly put down his napkin saying *That's it*, and stood up and left, followed by Frank. The waiter appeared with the check but the chauffeur did not make a move to handle it, so I finally said *We'd better pay the check now; my plane will leave soon.*

Yes, I guess we'd better, he said and just sat there. So I reached for the check and he finally came alert saying *maybe I had better pay that* and I said *Yes I think you'd better*. The chauffeur drove me to the plane and I flew back to Chino and the Pine Tree Motel.

I later learned from Harold Williams that Governor Brown's comment about me to Mario Oblato, Secretary of California's Health & Welfare Agency that had oversight over the Corrections Department, was that he did not like me. He said that I was too cocky and self confident, whereupon Mr. Oblato replied *You're talking about yourself, Governor, so you and Brook Carey should get along fine!*

He thought I was too self-confident? How could anyone head a large women's prison without having a significant measure of self-confidence? It did not make sense. (As reported by Dr. Joyce Brothers, "According to studies most American males admire confidence and self-respect in a woman. In fact, independence and self-confidence are qualities many males find sexy as well as intellectually stimulating. Their view is often that passive women are boring. Usually, males who demand passivity in women are themselves insecure.") I didn't speculate on where the Governor might fit into this observation.

The next day I called the Corrections Department and Harold Williams told me that even though the Governor did not like me, he had consented to my appointment. Harold said that next on my agenda was Senate confirmation scheduled for September 10. Appointed, not hired; serving at the pleasure of the Governor who did not like me! Now having to be confirmed by the Senate? Good Luck! Bill and I had a lengthy phone conversation that evening. He reassured me that in his experience getting along and fitting in with government and civilian bureaucracies are not very difficult when you play by the following rules: display self confidence, know what you're talking about, don't contest the system and always act slightly mysterious.

Orientation and Training

There was no operations manual for Prison Wardens. Harold Williams handed me a book, *Helter Skelter: The True Story of the Manson Murders* by Vincent Bugliosi and Curt Gentry. It is the story of the highest profile murders of the times (1969) by the hippie cult, Charles Manson "Family." He told me to read the book to learn about the Mansons. CIW had about a dozen high profile inmates, including four of the Manson "girls." Williams ordered that I personally was to make every decision regarding those high profile inmates. That was the primary direction that I got from my bosses at the Corrections Department.

Carlos Sanchez from the Corrections Department's Human Resources Department came to my rescue. He gave me an overview of the operations and administration of prisons by escorting me on visits to several men's prisons. We drove in his car and had ample time to talk along the way.

The first visit was at Folsom with Warden Jake Gunn. Jake was small in stature but tall in command presence. He was friendly in welcoming me. When he learned that I wanted to go into the prison yard with the inmates, he became nervous but acquiesced. I felt strangely empowered and was unafraid of this new experience. With an escort of six Correctional Officers, I walked confidently into the Folsom yard where hundreds of men were lounging and milling about. There was an undercurrent of low voices, almost sounding like a hum. The men looked at me curiously but kept their distance. We walked briskly to a nearby building where the license plate factory was located. It was interesting to see all the stamping machines and the paint booths. The stamping machines made deafening pounding noises so speech was impossible. As I passed through the factory, I smiled and mouthed "hello" to the inmates. Most of them grinned and waved. It was seldom that they saw a woman in the area, so I was a surprise to them.

As we passed through several more buildings, one of the Correctional Officers ran ahead to clear the way because the toilets are in the open and he wanted to spare me embarrassment. We did come across one man sitting on a toilet but I just looked the other way and kept walking. The entire Folsom circumstances were so overwhelming that getting embarrassed over a man on a toilet seemed superficial. I was given a complete tour, including the mess hall, the kitchen and the high security lockup unit. When I returned to Jake Gunn's office, he gripped my hands and said *I was so nervous that you were out there that I had to close my window blinds. Couldn't bear to watch. The last time a woman went into the yard, the inmates roughed her up. Glad you're safe!* I wondered why Jake hadn't warned me of the danger he had anticipated. I was just larking along with my escorts, as if taking a tour of a college campus. I had no thoughts of danger or dread.

Another interesting visit was at the California Correctional Center at Susanville where inmates are trained in firefighting. On our route driving to the prison Carlos and I became stopped by an unexpected snow storm while going through the pass at the top of the Sierra Nevada mountain range. The snow became so deep that we briefly entertained the possibility that we would have to sleep in the car overnight. That would have been difficult and awkward. The snow was over four feet deep and we sat for hours in a long line of cars waiting until the snowplows finally arrived to clear a narrow path.

The Susanville Warden was friendly too. When I asked to go into the yard, he summoned six members of the Inmate Council. *Mrs. Carey is the Superintendent of CIW*, he said. *Will you guarantee her safety if she goes into the yard with you?* The men were eager to oblige. Wearing a lemon-yellow wool pantsuit, I confidently walked into the yard where I sat on a cement bench awaiting developments. Hundreds of inmates circled the bench, staring at me. They came closer and closer then sat on the ground around me while my "guards" kept a watchful eye on the events. Soon, about fifty men were sitting by me and we began to talk. One man, a handsome African American with a shiny bald head, spoke first. *I am King Zodiac*, he said. *Aren't you afraid of us?* I answered boldly *I am Brook Carey, Superintendent of the women's prison at Frontera. Aren't you afraid of me?* That broke the ice and we began a discussion about prison life. I learned much from the prisoners' viewpoints that helped me relate to situations at CIW. We talked about how to improve the food service, what kinds of discipline were effective, what punishment was unacceptable, how to improve vocational training and education programs and much more. When I arrived back at CIW several days later there was a letter for me from King Zodiac. It was a fan letter of sorts. Of course I could not reply, but I was touched.

The Business Office

The financial affairs of CIW were under the stewardship of Scott Abbott, the Controller. He was in his forties, balding and wore large glasses—a mousey civil servant. He always told me there wasn't any money in the budget to do things I wanted to do. This fellow was really secretive. He played his cards close, but the answer was always *There isn't money in the budget.* During my initial tour of the facilities I was dismayed by the condition of his office. An overstuffed filing cabinet, loose files covering practically every horizontal surface including the seat of the one spare chair and an outdated calendar on the wall.

I made it a point to meet with him in my office when discussing budget matters. Whatever the subject was that I needed to discuss with him he invariably brought only a notebook and a few scraps of paper pertaining to the issue at hand. His excuse was that he was always too busy to prepare charts and graphs for my information. These encounters placed me somewhere between being angry and humiliated by his disrespect for my position and his indifference toward the prison. I realized early on that recruiting a new person to fill his position was imperative. I did not have a handle on my predecessor's budget but the picture brightened when I had a chance to prepare a budget of my own.

The California Legislature was using a sharp pencil when appropriations for the Corrections Department were planned and the women's prison was the last to be considered when passing out the funds. The American society in general is male supremacist so it is consistent that prisons mirror this social dynamic. Female offenders are confined in a system designed, built and run by men. Because the numbers of female felons are relatively low, there are no "economies of scale" in meeting their special needs. The Corrections Department seriously discriminated against CIW by not giving it enough staff, equipment and training. The underlying atmosphere was one of intense hostility, frustration and anger. It was an intolerable situation, unlike the male prisons. I felt frustrated by the status quo and vowed to become tuned in to the strategies to reverse that trend and permit CIW to get its fair share of goods and services.

My initial expectations of myself as the Warden were not significantly different from my attitude in other positions I had held. I was always confident that I would succeed at whatever challenge lay ahead. In the early days at CIW, I believed I could accomplish any task with ease; it was only a matter of time until I learned the ropes. The operations of the Corrections Department in Sacramento remained a mystery. For example, the Department would discover a problem, and then make a rule about it. The new rule might be completely opposite to an existing rule. I was accustomed to making a decision and working it out through negotiation or compromise but there seldom was a place for that in the Corrections system. There are rules that govern virtually everything. I could not go to war against the whole California criminal justice system. I would try to make their rules work, trying to understand the system. I was puzzled and frustrated that the skills that worked so well for me on the outside seemed out of place in the system.

I had not learned the maneuvers to get around the purchasing roadblocks but apparently people in the other prisons had. That is how those prisons managed to exist. I kept hearing about these activities so I mentioned it to the Warden of Soledad at the Wardens' meeting. He then sent his Deputy Warden to CIW for a week to help me evaluate my staff and scrounge for things we needed. I thought this could be the achievement of the year having this big man-mountain Deputy come down to help me. Almost immediately he intimidated my staff members and told me to terminate some of the poor performing individuals as soon as possible. I asked *How can I do that to civil service employees?* He chuckled. *That's easy, you just railroad them. I'll show you how.* Briefly I thought maybe I could really turn the place around with this man's help, but I was opposed to "railroading" anyone. Shortly after brief service to CIW, he was promoted to Warden of one of the men's prisons. At this point, I had learned some of the personnel tricks of the trade and started by having Scott transferred to CIM in Chino while recruiting another financial person who was better qualified and appeared to have more interest his work and the corrections system.

The State provided basic clothing so the residents who did not have financial resources were clothed. Most of the residents did have resources and brought in complete outfits and other clothing to supplement what was issued. Some of the residents ordered items from Neiman Marcus and other top of the line mail order stores. One resident wanted to buy gifts for other residents from Neiman Marcus. That was difficult to assess, because we did not know if she was buying favors or dealing in something illegal. We investigated and learned that on the outside she did have a large bank account, and she wanted to dress in high class clothing and share items from upscale stores.

The types of items that were ordered from shopping catalogs and delivered to residents were almost overwhelming. Before my arrival, the administration was so permissive that residents could send for almost anything they wanted. The residents had to have their Correctional Counselors' permissions for the orders, what these are and where these are coming from. On one occasion, a resident wanted to order $8,000 worth of merchandise ($31,500 in 2008 funds) so I had to give permission also. All packages coming into CIW had to be carefully searched, putting an additional strain on our shortage of Correctional Officers.

I began to get complaints about the prison-issue clothing and of course I plunged in to investigate. This was something that I could readily understand. CIW's commercial laundry had many large machines operated by residents. They ran the bras and rayon underpants through the washers and dryers along with the work clothes, so of course flimsy lingerie did not last long. CIW had a position of Storekeeper II, a warehouse person reporting to the Business Office, filled by a young man who used to be an office clerk now industriously working his way up. I saw the sleazy underwear that he had been buying, and I knew that we weren't getting our money's worth. Women's underwear was something I could relate to.

I had a talk with the young man in charge of the store room. *Next time the salesman from the underwear company comes to CIW, let me know so I can meet with him.* The salesman arrived a few weeks later with a sample case filled with all types of women's underwear, pink lacey things and the shoddy stuff that is sold in budget stores. Samples of panties were strung all over a display area. It was a comical scene. Staff members came by while this was going on. The subject of buying underwear seemed to be titillating to all the male staff members. *What are you into now, Mrs. Carey?* I remember the staff members thought it was a frivolous morning.

I selected the grade of underpants and brassieres that were a better quality. I learned that bright pink, blue, green and yellow underpants were more expensive, so I ordered all white underwear of a better quality. This really annoyed the residents; they wanted bright colors. The residents liked raucous colors and the sleazier the better. I thought the residents would be happy having serviceable underwear that wasn't raveling and having the elastic coming out. I selected the kind of underwear that I might buy for myself, well made without lace. I was certain that any lace trim would not make it through the industrial washing machines. I was unaware that not giving them colored sleazy underpants would ruin their day. The negative response to my well-meaning actions was upsetting and I determined to become more informed before jumping into situations.

One resident, Josephine, had enormous breasts and a brassiere large enough to fit her was not available through the purchasing system. She endlessly complained that she needed to go outside the prison and be fitted by a corsetiere. I took one look at her and realized she was right. She would be going out on parole in another month and I knew that this was an important issue with her. She felt that she could not face the world without a proper fitting brassiere. I arranged for a female Corrections Officer to drive her to a store for oversize women in town. Josephine was properly fitted and when she returned to CIW, she took great delight in lifting her T-shirt to display the ample brassiere we found for her. I was happy that my intercession had been a success.

Security and Custody

All of the women sent to CIW were felons. A felon is defined as a person who commits a crime punishable by more than one year of incarceration, not further specified. So people who have committed a nonspecific crime carrying a sentence of more than one year are considered to be felons and go to State prison. If the sentence is less than a year, they go to the County jail.

One of the large rooms in the Administration Building was the records office. Many file cabinets were piled high around the room. Three clerks worked steadily to keep abreast of the paperwork that accumulated for each resident. There were fat folders of information on every resident but there were too few hours in my day to examine them all during my tenure. I estimate I read about one hundred folders in depth, including those of the dozen high profile residents that I was required to handle personally. I did not know who most of the residents were; they did not wear numbers or badges. Their faces were a blur to me. We discussed making residents wear name badges, but then they would have switched badges or stolen each other's badges. It was more trouble and expense than it was worth.

Residents were not locked in their rooms during the day unless they were being disciplined. They were free to walk about on the campus and in the buildings. This made security quite difficult. I tried to establish identification cards with residents' names and photos, what programs they were in and what custody level they were. But the staff members told me they had almost every resident memorized. CIW was a <u>minimum</u> security facility but it had three levels of custody: minimum, medium, and maximum security. The maximum security residents are locked in their rooms after dinner; minimums and mediums may come out after dinner and sit outside or attend a movie; they weren't required to show any ID. Residents were required to be in their rooms at 7:00 A.M., 1:00 P.M., 7:00 P.M. and 1:00 A.M. to be counted. We quickly would know if any resident had escaped or was hiding somewhere within the campus.

Heading the custody function was Deputy Superintendent, Ron Burke. He acted as if he had commanded military troops before, so I had faith in his experience. Sadly, Ron initially was not trusted by the residents because they saw him as a "big fist" from Folsom Prison. Anything he did was suspicious as far as the residents were concerned. He worked hard to earn their confidence and became more effective in his job.

Custody was a paramilitary function with an echelon of Correctional Officers, Sergeants, Lieutenants and a Captain. The previous Superintendent decreed that they did not have to wear uniforms. This was a problem for me because I could not tell female Correctional Officers from the residents. I soon reinstituted the requirement to wear uniforms. At CIW we had 200 Correctional Officers on the roster, but because of sick leave and vacation time to use, there seldom was more than seventy five percent of the correctional staff available for duty at any one time.

There are many dangerous people incarcerated in prisons and they have weapons fashioned inside or smuggled from the outside. Virtually all of my staff members risked their lives daily but they did not carry weapons. Because of the bureaucracy and how rigid it is, many of the entry-level Correctional Officers were minimally qualified. And being union members and civil service employees, terminating poor performers was difficult. Some of the minimum security <u>residents</u> I relied upon to do work within the prison were better qualified than the entry level Correctional Officers employed at that time.

After a few weeks, I began to relax in terms of worrying about my personal safety. I realized that no resident would "leap out at me with a weapon" when I walked on campus. Staff members were skilled in keeping the prison culture calm. Most of the residents in CIW were not especially dangerous to the staff members because endless hours were spent working with residents. Unlike men's prisons where staff members control inmates physically, CIW's methods of talking, cajoling and reasoning were the most effective control mechanisms with women. I became personally acquainted with dozens of residents and enjoyed working with them. Some of these are described later in this book.

Madge Culver was the Captain of the Correctional Officers, working directly for Ron Burke. She was a petite and attractive redhead. In spite of her small stature, she was dynamic! She had an extensive background in Corrections, had worked in Paroles, had been a Correctional Officer, and was recently was promoted to Captain. Madge had never commanded anyone in a paramilitary organization before, anymore than I had, but at least she knew how the Corrections system worked and had her head on straight. She was one of our really experienced staff members. Madge usually had a broad smile. She was easy to supervise and always pulled more than her weight. I liked her immediately and relied upon her to keep me informed of goings-on within the prison. She always gave me a straight story, unlike some other staff members. She later became the Warden of two of the men's prisons and enjoyed a very successful career in Corrections.

Around the perimeter of CIW were about five small buildings instead of watchtowers. These looked like outhouses and were unarmed. When a resident made an escape attempt by climbing over the perimeter fence, the only action the unarmed Officers could take was to shout or try to tackle them. That is why a number of residents were easily able to escape over the fence the previous year. Citizens think that they're paying $12,000 per year (1975 dollars) per woman to keep her in prison. That was a large sum in 1975, and for what? Protecting society from that individual? Yes, but the bureaucrats did not help me keep the residents in the prison. When I put armed Correctional Officers on the perimeter I was astonished to learn that these Correctional Officers did not know how to handle weapons and under civil service I could not make them take the weapons qualifications training. I selected those that already knew how to handle weapons and armed the perimeter. Then the "brass" said *Do not shoot at anyone. We never have shot at a female felon and no one is authorized to shoot at one now.* Of course the residents knew that.

Every California prison has at least one Correctional Officer specifically assigned to "Security" (Intelligence.) Ron Burke recruited a friend of his from CIM. This person was a Correctional Officer (Lieutenant) named Red Wilson. Red was gung-ho in the prison gang intelligence business. That was his hobby, knowing who all the offenders were and tracking them and their relationships. When he came to work at CIW, he brought with him his gang files and interest in prison gang activities. When there is a staff member 100% interested in prison gang activity, chances are there will be a lot of prison gang activity. In retrospect, it appears Red may have created this activity through his own interest.

In most prisons the position is called Investigation Lieutenant and Red Wilson had filled that function in a number of California prisons. However, CIW was not authorized to have that position because we were understaffed, without enough Correctional Officers. So Red had to serve as a Correctional Officer Lieutenant and work a regular shift. I became the defacto Investigation Lieutenant under his tutoring. Red was convinced that CIW was under a great threat from the prison gangs because many of our residents were married to or connected to gang members in the men's prisons.

It was very interesting to work with Red and I became very involved in his interests. I became embroiled in "intelligence" and became a minor expert about the prison gangs. I could speak with authority about them. Red was proud of my knowledge and invited me to come to special monthly meetings of all the gumshoe investigative people: FBI, police, correctional people and sheriff's department. This was an in-group that few knew existed and I was privileged to be invited. This group provided liaison with the prisons. We had a constant information exchange. The group told Red that CIW was the central focus of communications for all the gangs: the Black Guerilla Family, the Mexican Mafia, Nuestra Familia, the Arian Brotherhood, etc. Ron Burke was tuned into the prison gang system politically and perhaps he took advantage of my lack of experience. Both Ron and Red, coming from Folsom and CIM, may have felt that CIW was a "cream puff" assignment. Catching prison gangs was a "tough" activity so perhaps Ron and Red felt they had to make sure there was gang activity for them to suppress. If I was prepared to gather intelligence at CIW, I would be the first one to learn of any gang activity or any gang bust at the men's prisons. I was confident that I was going to catch any type of this activity in the act at CIW. I felt excited at the prospect of that.

Residents are permitted to write letters to anyone. The rule states that when a letter is written by an inmate to the State Legislature or to the Governor, staff members may not read it. If it goes to a legitimate member of public service, it is not to be read. So that was the favorite game, firing off letters to officials detailing real or imagined shortcomings of the prison and its staff. A great deal of our time was spent reacting to investigations that were initiated by the recipients of these letters. Lieutenant Madge was amused by my investigative efforts. *Brook, haven't you got enough paperwork to handle without letting Red drag you into his "hobby"?* But I was intrigued by the possibility of performing a great coup d'état and ignored her comments.

I was supposed to read all the incoming and outgoing mail of the residents who were suspected of gang activity. Those residents used to play "games" with us just because they knew we were reading their letters. They would write things to waste our time. A written prison expression is the word "smile." For example, a resident would write "today I went to my job in the kitchen, smile, and I went to bed early, smile" etc. The word "smile" is used like a comma. Some outside correspondents would draw smiley ☺ faces that were coated with LSD after the word "smile" so residents could lick the faces on the paper and get a minor high. Frequently I saw suspicious things in the letters and Red then interviewed the residents involved and reported the results to me.

There were certain residents referred to as "snitches." When they were able, they would call us on the interoffice telephone system and give us information. They did it because prison is a frightening place to be. We knew who the snitches were but they never talked to us openly, and we never called them into our offices. It was dangerous to be a snitch so their identities were carefully guarded. Once, we received a snitch call that a weapon was hidden in the Administration Building. After a time-consuming search, one-half of a large scissors with a taped handle was found stashed in the fire alarm box just outside my office door. At home that night I was jubilant. *Hey, Bill. The staff found a taped half of scissors in the fire alarm box outside my office door.* Bill looked quizzical and replied *Did they find the other half?* I hadn't thought about that. But surprisingly, I didn't feel any fear or dread. Maybe I was getting numb to the dangers of the prison culture. That other half scissors never turned up.

Various groups of residents came and went in power at CIW such as the Arian Sisterhood group. Those residents were the wives or girlfriends of men in prison who were in the Arian Brotherhood gang. Many of those men were Hells Angels bikers. The Arian Sisters kept quietly to themselves. Their actions were behind the scenes manipulating other groups. The Arian Sisterhood was the only group that I think really did exist at CIW. I do not think we had the Black Guerilla Family or the Mexican Mafia or Nuestra Familia activity. The Hispanic residents were a mystery to me, because I had never before encountered the Mexican culture. However, many of the Hispanic residents at CIW were aggressive and dangerous, not mild mannered.

The Mothers Anonymous group consisted of about forty residents whose offense was killing their children. A volunteer psychiatrist came twice a week to work with them. Several trouble makers found spray paint cans and wrote on the sidewalks and the side of the Education building, "Kill the Baby Killers." The Mothers Anonymous members were terrified and demanded to be placed in protective custody. At CIW protective custody meant an isolation cell in the Psychiatric Treatment Unit (PTU) with no TV or comforts. We did not have enough protective custody cells for all of them so many of those residents became out of control. Imagine forty residents screaming hysterically, wanting protective custody, and only twenty protective custody available cells. This was a pathetic group; one of the saddest things that I encountered at CIW. Luckily, the threats turned out to be empty and the situation cooled down in a few weeks. Meanwhile, we doubled the custody staff members in their cottage to maintain an increased watch over those frightened residents.

One form used for a disciplinary report that any employee of the prison could write on any resident for an infraction of the rules was called a 115. These are used to document a major offense that must be investigated and sometimes prosecuted. A lesser offense is written as a 128A. The big "game" was for any infraction, the staff members would say "I'm going to write you up" and they would write up a 115. Then the resident would try to argue it down to a 128A.

There were strict policies governing the processing of 115s. The rule was that the circumstances surrounding the writing of a 115 must be investigated promptly by staff members. One of the staff would be appointed as an investigating officer to represent the resident. The gardeners, the cooks, the garbage man—every employee had to take a turn being an investigating officer. About thirty percent of a staff member's time was consumed with the investigations of 115s. We would have up to forty 115s a day. We could hardly get any other work done. After the investigation by an employee, a panel of other staff members would be convened for a hearing with the resident and the investigator. Then it would be decided if the 115 was deserved or if it should be cancelled or modified to a 128A.

Ron Burke was in charge of resolving the 115s and the 128As. It was virtually all he had time to do so he scarcely could get the custody people together, trained, organized, staffed or positioned. Of course, in hindsight, I should have disciplined the staff members for writing too many 115s for mostly minor infractions. It was easier for them to write a 115 than it was to figure out how to deal with the infraction. Ron appeared to take exception to it when I asked to review some of the 115s. I was trying to get a handle on the situation and to learn what was going on. Ron would leave 115s on my desk for a day or two, and then stop giving them to me. He counted on the fact that I would be buried in other paperwork and would not have time to follow up. That was business as usual. I was so busy with busy work that I scarcely had time to feel anger or resentment. I was concerned that I wasn't "cutting it" because the paperwork was so overwhelming so I just kept my head down and plowed through my pile of work.

In prison there are many small infractions, and if you're not a skilled people-person, it is easier to write up a 115 than to deal with the problem. This was how the staff members showed their authority over the residents who could not be paroled if they had too many write-ups in their files. At that time, the State of California used "indeterminate" sentencing. Felons had no way to know how long their sentences would be. The Parole Board had been influenced by the staff members to judge those write ups and use them as a rationale for keeping residents from receiving a parole. To counter this, I created a cross file of the 115s by staff members who issued them and every month I reviewed how many they had generated and for what reasons. I began to regulate certain staff members who were failing to deal with problems. This greatly reduced the investigation time and helped to bring us back to more challenging custody activities.

I literally was trying to go by the rule book. As a law-abiding citizen I thought there must be sense to all this. It did not occur to me that maybe I was not the incompetent one, that maybe some of the management in the Corrections Department was incompetent. I was ineffective because the system was set up to operate only one way—inefficiently. I had no experience with paramilitary hierarchy and political appointments. I had to comply with many rigid and impractical rules and do that within certain time deadlines. For example, a thick book would arrive in the mail from the Corrections Department with orders to complete an extensive survey. Deputy Superintendent Ron Burke was so bogged down with his primary duties that he had little time to become involved in "make work" projects originating in Sacramento.

I was trying to work within a system that was in shambles. I thought everything that went wide of the mark was my fault, either by commission or omission. I believed I had to be literal in enforcing the rules, to demonstrate to the residents that rules are meant to be obeyed. I believed that the rules could not be bent or ignored. It took me a while to learn from other Wardens that there were ways to work around some of them.

I saw myself as a symbol of the law. That was my job and I was sworn by the Senate to uphold the rules, no matter how I felt about them. Governor Brown's instructions to me, "Keep the inmates in there, and keep them healthy" mandated that my priorities focus on custody and medical matters, when actually I'm a rehabilitation person. Being one of the highest paid women in California civil service was a weighty experience. And being the only one who came into management at CIW without advancing through the ranks, I was a peculiarity and got much more than my share of the attention. The spotlight was on me to succeed or fail in front of the entire correctional system. Privately I worried that I would fail because I had to deal with so many unknowns, and my management style appeared to be ill-suited to the Corrections bureaucracy. I resolved to try to become attuned to the bureaucratic style. Success in this job meant everything to me.

It was trying times like these, particularly when Bill was still back in Michigan and my evening routines revolved around the Pine Tree Motel that I wondered if I had made a mistake in accepting the appointment. Not only was this testing my resolve but it rekindled my thoughts of Bill when he was serving in Korea and Viet Nam facing challenge after challenge while relying on the warmth and comfort of memories of home and an occasional short wave telephone patch to his loved ones.

Disciplinary Lockup

The Psychiatric Treatment Unit (PTU) was a separate building that had a security fence completely surrounding it. It had a kitchen, dining room, classrooms and individual rooms for psychiatric residents housed there. One wing of PTU was used to lock residents in cells temporarily for disciplinary reasons, usually for less than one week. In the disciplinary wing, the cells had a bunk and a toilet. When a resident was put in lockup, all her clothing was removed and she was given a type of housedress gown and rubber thongs. She had no undergarments in the cell. According to staff members this was because many residents in lockup are really angry, thrashing and trashing and ripping the toilets off the wall. We had to ensure they did not hang themselves with their bra or stuff their panties down the toilet, or use their shoes to hit someone. Later, I came to learn that taking their clothing was done primarily to humiliate them.

Most of the residents in lockup had been acting out, kicking and screaming so violently that they had to be locked up. That is why the lockup unit is called the "cooler." It provided an environment in which the resident could regain some self control. Undoubtedly the staff members could have been more discerning when deciding what frame of mind a resident was in. This would have allowed some residents to keep their clothing and shoes. If any resident was in lockup for more than two days, staff members brought her a toothbrush and other personal items.

It was my practice to visit this lockup unit at least every other day to check on those residents. I learned that staff members were locking up residents and sometimes were apparently too busy to follow up. The result was that those in lockup did not get their hearings in a timely way. It was drafty and cold in there and offered nothing to read or do. The California Rehabilitation Center (CRC) in nearby Corona housed both men and women with drug problems but did not have punitive cells. When a woman at CRC would act up, she would be transported to CIW for detention in our lockup unit. This only added to our under staffed and underfunded burdens.

Every morning, a Corrections Officer and the residents' Counselors were supposed to review why a resident was in lockup and make a determination about the duration of her stay. It was like an unofficial court proceeding. If the resident was showing hostility and a bad attitude, the Correctional Officer would say *We'll take a look at you tomorrow and see how you're feeling—Next case!*

I took a great interest in those residents when I discovered the daily reviews were not happening for some of them. The staff members would get busy handling other matters and forget to do the reviews. I sensed that some staff members would have liked to keep the trouble makers locked up indefinitely. Many times before I left at night, I would visit the PTU lockup and walk down the hall, speaking through the bars to each woman there. The residents appreciated my concern. The word got around campus that the Superintendent frequently checked on the residents in the lockup, personally talking to each one.

Initially, I was under the impression that the residents in the lockup unit were the worst trouble makers so I sat in on a review to see for myself. The first resident to be reviewed was Marguerite. She'd been in a fight with another resident. Marguerite had never been in trouble before, but I did not know this at the time. I assumed that I was meeting the worst of the worst. Ron Burke chaired the review and Marguerite's Counselor was there along with the head of the lockup unit and me. We met in a closet-size room with no air conditioning; there wasn't even space to sit down. There were four of us and the resident, so it was really uncomfortable. I did not observe anything particularly dangerous about Marguerite. She was weeping, her long false eyelashes were crooked and she was disheveled. I later learned that she was enrolled in the LVN nurses' program. Being in lockup was interfering with her working in that program and was contributing to her distress.

Marguerite, tell me about the fight I said. *How long have you been in lockup?* She was startled that the Superintendent was speaking during this review but began to relate her story. She caught another resident in her room, rummaging through her things. Upon being confronted, the other resident started the fight. She had been in lockup three days and appeared ready to be released. After a brief discussion, the group agreed that Marguerite had "cooled down" and could go back to her cottage. I took an immediate liking to Marguerite and looked forward to encountering her and getting to know her. I thought to myself as I walked back to my office that this was justice done in a fair and reasonable manner but I, Brook, was not able to be personally involved in every single incident involving the fair and just treatment of a resident. This is where the art of delegation comes in if there is anyone to whom I can delegate with confidence. This really is a formidable job! But I am feeling more confident of handling it and growing with it.

Counseling and Social Services

The staff member who supervised the counseling and social services was a tall, handsome African American named Allen Brown, also a Deputy Superintendent. He never was called Allen or Mr. Brown; he was called AllenBrown—one word. In the prison, the residents had to refer to all staff members as Miss, Mrs. Mr. preceding their names. He did not like that and simply preferred to be called "AllenBrown." I was impressed with AllenBrown. He was articulate, intelligent and interesting. He would wheel and deal to get his job done. He was in charge of visitors and outside groups that came into CIW and all the Correctional Counselors and social activities within the prison. His methods notwithstanding, he did an excellent job.

AllenBrown had received his training outside of Prisons and he needed Institutional experience to move up in the prison system. He was employed initially as a social worker and then moved into the Parole system. He was being groomed for advancement. Popular with the residents, he often was on their side against the staff members. He talked "Ebonese" with the African American residents, and interpreted for me. Many residents regarded him as their friend, so he was one of our best communication links to the campus intrigues and activities.

The Correctional Counselors reporting to AllenBrown consisted of two men and six women with backgrounds in social work. They provided "group therapy" and individual counseling. Their offices were located off the day rooms, or the lounges, of the cottages. They were instructed to be in or around their offices in case a resident had a problem. They also were to work one-on-one with residents who were exhibiting unusual stress or who needed intense rehabilitation, correction or advising. Weekly, the Correctional Counselors would hold what was called "the groups". They tried to provide group therapy with about seventy residents in a group. I was told by some residents that group therapy was a technique whereby they "put down" a resident in front of everyone in the group. Those techniques were not used when I attended these sessions. Each time I observed a group session, my presence seemed too much of a distraction. These sessions did serve to reinforce a sometimes fragile counselor/resident relationship.

The Correctional Counselors appeared buried in paperwork. While required to make reports to the Parole Board they also had to document continuing evaluations of each resident. Although the Correctional Counselors gave me their work-ups for review and signature, it was difficult to figure out exactly what guidelines and preparation went in their work-ups. Too often, they appeared to be generating 'rubber stamp' work-ups. The Counselors needed to be intimately familiar with up to one hundred residents in their case loads. That notwithstanding, there must have been a better way to provide one-on-one attention for residents with deeper problems. AllenBrown did his best to make a fractured system look like a positive endeavor.

An unforgettable Counselor was Floyd Rifkin. He resembled the actor Elliot Gould with a large, black frizzy hairstyle. His hefty stomach hung over his pants. Floyd liked to wear silky, body-fitted sport shirts. The bottom two buttons were usually undone and he'd sit in meetings with his hairy stomach and navel on display. I reprimanded him about it several times until finally, I became impatient saying *Floyd, if I see your belly button one more time, I am going to terminate you!*

Floyd Rifkin was married to one of the Correctional Officers, who was as beautiful as a model. It was difficult to imagine why such an attractive woman would be married to "Mr. Gross Belly." Actually, Floyd had the best academic credentials of all the Correctional Counselors, so he was assigned to work in the Psychiatric Treatment Unit (PTU). He also was the Counselor to the Manson girls and worked with other challenging cases. He was quite effective with this group. I kept trying to work with him and I wondered why I could not see the entire worth of this fellow.

One day I got a phone call from Floyd saying he'd lost his keys. For a prison staff member to lose keys is a major offense. I was so apprehensive about not losing mine that I kept them on an elastic wrist bracelet so I could not put them down by accident. After an intensive and secretive search that did not turn up the keys, every door and gate had to be quickly re-keyed in the event a resident may have come upon them. Changing prison keys is a complex task. Professional locksmiths from Chino were summoned to work with our full-time locksmith. It took many days and cost a great deal of money that could have been used in many other ways. I informed Floyd his careless act would be documented in his personnel file and would be considered at his evaluation time.

Before I came to CIW, Floyd and his wife had worked closely with one of the residents. After she was paroled, she then made them beneficiaries in her will. Several months later she was killed in an automobile accident. We got word that some members of our staff had inherited a great deal of money. We learned further that a former resident was the sole heiress to her parents' assets. They had had died a month before she died in her fatal accident. Floyd and his wife were about to receive hundreds of thousands of dollars. He must have been an effective Counselor to be awarded in that manner.

Another counselor, Larry Watson, was an African American with a great smile and a wonderful sense of humor. His head was totally bald, and shiny. There were many jokes about Larry: your head is shining in my eyes and words like that. He was effective with many of the residents who perceived him as a warm fatherly type of guy; he had Caucasian, African American and Hispanic residents in his case load and he got along well with all of them.

There was a position called Program Administrator. I had two of them; one for the main campus and one for the Psychiatric Treatment Unit and Reception Center. When I was appointed as Superintendent, the Program Administrator for the main campus was Belle Rowan, a talented African American woman about fifty-five with a Master's degree in Sociology. She had been with the system for several years. I had high respect for her and thought she was one of the best staff people at CIW. When I attended the summer Wardens' Meeting, I met the Director of Corrections from Nevada who was attending our meeting. He asked if I knew of a qualified candidate to become the Warden of the Nevada Women's Prison and I immediately recommended Belle Rowan. I was pleased to learn of her subsequent selection for that position but realized that I had "shot myself in the foot." Nevada Corrections recruited a real prize because Belle was virtually irreplaceable.

CIW had a unit called the Reception Center (RC). Prior to sentencing, judges sent convicted women to the RC for evaluation. The Correctional Counselors and Correctional Officers supervised the women in the RC. There were women to be evaluated from all over the State and some from other States as well. They would arrive by bus and be escorted into the RC, which also was guarded by a locked gate from the main campus. The women would stay in the RC for orientation and evaluations. Within ninety days, the RC staff members would decide what to do with them and release them back to the courts for sentencing. Some of the women had already been sentenced, so they would be released to the campus if that was indicated. I received a daily report about who was released and who came onto the campus, but these women generally were only names to me unless there was a high profile crime on their record.

The Manson "Girls"

As my boss, Walt Cooper, had instructed me, I was to personally make every decision concerning a dozen notorious residents at CIW. I read their case histories and I knew about their offenses. The most infamous of these dozen were the Manson "girls," Susan Atkins, Mary Brunner (Charlie Manson's common-law wife), Patricia Krenwinkle and Leslie Van Houten.

The girls were in their late teens when they joined Charles Manson's hippie-like cult. Cult-members indulged in drugs, and popular culture may have influenced their acts, especially a song by the Beatles, "Helter Skelter." This song inspired Manson to attempt to provoke a race war in the United States. In August 1969, Manson sent out his followers on two nights of gruesome murders. Their first target was the home of actress Sharon Tate who, along with her unborn child and four others, was slain. The second round of murders was in the home of Mr. and Mrs. Gino LaBianca who owned a grocery business. Leslie Van Houten was not present at the Tate slayings, but went along with Susan Atkins and Patricia Krenwinkle the following night to the LaBianca home. The three girls were convicted of the murders and sentenced to death. Their sentences were commuted to life in prison when California's death penalty was briefly overturned in the 1970s.

The girls and Mary Brunner were housed at CIW apart from the general population in a small building on the campus. AllenBrown escorted me to meet them. They had been under the influence of heavy drugs when living with Charlie and the drugs had influenced their actions. Now drug-free, they were friendly and appeared to be cooperative, normal young women. AllenBrown recommended that they be permitted to join the general population and be assigned to school and jobs. I concurred and they were released from the small building soon thereafter. They were model prisoners, trying to "do their time" quietly, out of sight of the media.

Susan Atkins appeared to be more affected by previous drug use than the other two girls. At CIW she had several intense religious experiences that caused her to switch from adoration of Charlie Manson to adoration of Jesus. She related that it seemed her room door opened and a brilliant white light poured over her. Jesus appeared to her and told her she was forgiven. Jesus then became virtually her total life. She made a deliberate break from the "Family" and moved to a different cottage on the campus.

Making music is a therapeutic pastime so I was pleased to support Susan's interest in building a dulcimer from a kit she had ordered. A dulcimer is a fretted string instrument of the zither family, typically with three or four strings, although contemporary versions of the instrument can have as many as twelve strings and six courses. The dulcimer body extends the length of the fingerboard and traditionally has an hourglass, teardrop, triangular or elliptical shape. When the instrument was finished, Bill and I shopped several music stores in town to purchase dulcimer music books. Staff members may not give gifts to residents, so we donated the music books to the CIW Library for Susan to use. Susan enjoyed playing her new instrument and became skilled with it.

Susan also had a significant artistic talent and enjoyed drawing with pastels. In early 1975, she completed a History class through Chaffey College, receiving a grade of B. Her Counselor stated that "Susan is a pleasant appearing young woman, who relates to her peers with warmth and friendliness."

Susan continues to be denied parole. In 2008, she will be sixty years old. At each denial, the parole board primarily cites the gravity of her crime, the fact that the murders were carried out in an especially cruel and callous manner. At the last Hearing, I learned that Susan listened without reaction and then was escorted out of the Hearing room with no protest.

Patricia Krenwinkle kept mostly to herself. It was hard to read what was going on with her. She maintained a perfect prison record. I noticed that she had excessive body hair and I tried to persuade an endocrinologist from Loma Linda Hospital to check on her. Nothing came of that because no such doctor could be found to volunteer his services. Patricia enrolled in the college program and later received a college degree. She later became active in prison support programs focused on alcohol and drug abuse. She worked also with fellow prisoners teaching them how to read.

Leslie Van Houten was attractive and outgoing. She was close with her family who continued to work actively for her freedom. I spoke several times on the telephone to her mother and encouraged her to try all avenues to help Leslie. In early 1976 her conviction briefly was reversed when the Court of Appeal ordered a new trial for her because her case had not been separated from her co-defendants when her attorney, Ronald Hughes, disappeared late in the proceedings.

While Leslie was out on bail awaiting the new trial, Mrs. Van Houten invited me to join her, Leslie and the Editor of the *Los Angeles Times* for lunch at the

Dorothy Chandler Pavilion in Los Angeles. As we sat at the table, Leslie said *Mrs. Carey wouldn't our waiter be surprised if he knew who we are?* Indeed! The purpose of the meeting was to discuss ways to help Leslie earn her freedom. I was in favor of that because the Leslie of 1975 was an entirely different person from the drugged hippie of the Manson Family days. While at CIW, Leslie earned two college degrees and is a model inmate. I believe that the new Leslie is not a danger to anyone and that she should be permitted to earn her freedom. The Parole Board apparently disagreed. In spite of an "exemplary" prison record that spans over thirty-five years, Leslie was turned down for the sixteenth time in August 2006.

Mary Brunner filed a lawsuit against me because she was locked in her room at night, as were all the residents. This was just another nuisance to combat. Of course she lost the suit. Can you imagine what would happen to the Corrections system if Mary won her case? Keeping felons in locked cells is the heart of Corrections in most states.

Susan, Patricia and Leslie always were very friendly toward me. They appreciated that I was closely involved in making decisions that affected them but I felt they sincerely liked me for myself. I tried to reflect that same friendly informality when I talked with them.

(At publication date, Leslie, Patricia and Susan remain at Frontera. Mary was paroled years ago.)

Food Service

Food Service in a prison is a high priority. Connie Wade, who headed the Food Service at the Village Cafeteria, was a plump sixty-year old dietician with bleached blonde hair piled high. She was terrified by the residents and seldom emerged from her office. She hid in her office so she would not have to confront the problems with food preparation, menus and food service. The result was that food was unappetizing. The same limited menus were offered. The kitchen was unclean; everything was in disarray. The kitchen workers were residents, except for a few supervisory staff members. Connie had to depend mainly on the residents to get the jobs done. This put her in a position of being dependent upon the good will of the residents who worked for her but she did not know how to earn that good will, and residents had total command of the kitchen. The hard truth is that people who are afraid of inmates cannot work in prisons. She was a graduate dietician but she certainly did not show imagination about the food service.

For example, when I arrived at CIW residents would be served slabs of bologna and mounds of bread in a wrapper. One morning, we had a near riot in the Village Cafeteria because the food was so unappealing. Another day there was a demonstration because a resident picked up a worm from her plate of baked beans. *There's a worm in my food!* She began screaming and throwing her food as the residents joined in throwing their food. We figured out later that she planted the worm, because when we eventually found it, it was a raw worm that she'd brought in from a plot of soil on the campus.

One of the residents called Ace was a consistent trouble maker about the food. She was an African American in her early twenties, a solid 6 foot 2 inches tall, about 280 lbs. Ace always complained that she was hungry, but she did not look malnourished. Her complaint about not enough food had absolutely no merit. Residents were encouraged to eat all the fruit, vegetables and bread they wanted. Only one entrée was permitted, however. When I would take a visitor into the campus, Ace would inevitably come up to us when I was with one of the "big shots" and say, "I'm hungry, I ain't gettin' enough to eat. The food in this place …" and she'd go on about everything wrong with the food service program.

Sometimes, the visitor would become official saying "Maybe we should go to the dining area and investigate this." With an Assemblyman or other highly placed political visitor, you just do not say "No, you can't go to the mess halls." Ace loved to make problems for me with officials and I felt annoyed at her whenever she approached me. Because of Ace's low I.Q. it was difficult to reason with her. She frequently beat up residents, keeping them frightened. Often when residents came from the Canteen with candy bars and sodas; Ace would steal from them, or intimidate them. We seldom could catch her in the act so usually she escaped discipline.

As complaints about the food increased, I had to take action. I called Connie into my office. *I'm sorry, but you can't work here anymore. You're afraid of the residents so you'd better stay out of the prison food service business.* I persuaded her to take a leave of absence. I quickly found a replacement for her and started a Vocational Food Service Program, described in a later chapter.

Education

There were two teachers employed at CIW. Martin Murphy was a schoolteacher, acting as principal of our schools. He was a fellow the residents liked to flirt with. To women who did not have a man in their lives, he was attractive. He was about forty-six, a man not quite looking me in the eyes. Martin had been divorced a couple of times and I thought he might be a problem in a woman's prison. I never had any specific reason to be concerned but I wasn't sure what to make of him.

Working for him as the other teacher was Rosalyn Levin, a plumpish woman who was extremely bright. She was a Registered Nurse who had left nursing and had established a Licensed Vocational Nurse (LVN) program in the prison. A busload of residents was driven out of the prison daily into local community hospitals where they trained as LVNs. Many of these residents eventually passed the State exam and earned their LVN licenses. This was an avant-garde program for a prison. Rosalyn was somewhat annoying, talkative, biting her nails and twisting her hair while darting around. The LVN program required a registered nurse to supervise it, so when I felt irritated with her; I realized if I terminated her, the program would be ended.

The residents enrolled in the LVN program formed a cohesive group and because they were classified as minimum custody, were free to live together in the same cottage and to plan recreational activities together. One afternoon, Ron Burke notified me that one of the LVN trainees had not boarded the return bus at the required time and therefore was classified as missing and unaccounted for. He had notified the Chino Police and an All Points Bulletin was issued.

He said that the other trainees were assembled in the Education Building with Rosalyn so I hurried to the classroom to meet with them. What a sorry sight! Huddled together, the residents were weeping and whispering. It took some cajoling to get their attention and settle them down. The major concern was that the trainees feared I would cancel the program. Actually, that course of action had not occurred to me. I trusted these residents and assured them that the program would continue. They were relieved to know that I did not favor mass punishment. That evening the Watch Commander received a phone call from the missing LVN trainee who stated she had become so involved with a gravely ill patient that she missed the bus. A Correctional Officer was dispatched to return her to CIW. When it came time for her disciplinary hearing I made it a point to sit in on the proceedings. It was determined that while using poor judgment, she had no intent to escape. She would be able to continue her LVN training while giving up certain campus privileges for several weeks.

We offered kindergarten through twelfth grade classes and some college credit courses. After testing, most residents were about at a sixth grade level. The most popular course in CIW was "Bonehead" English, where residents learned to write and spell. It was taught by faculty from Chaffee College located in Alta Loma. It was a night class, and students from Chaffey came to CIW so we could make up a full class. We had several other classes such as history and geography from Chaffey. Initially, I was concerned about the custody of the residents, because of teachers and students coming in from the outside but there were no problems. Residents going to college lived together in one of the cottages and that became the "elite" group on the campus.

Aside from the Chaffee program, some of the teachers were civil service employees, on contracts for nine months each year. The contracts were supervised through the Board of Education of the Chino School District. Each resident had a schedule or an activity. Kindergarten was for those who were illiterate or did not speak English. The Chino Board had free rein to decide which teachers would participate in these programs. I believed we had teachers who were teaching the Hispanic residents how to speak English as a second language, and surprisingly it just wasn't happening. They remained tongue tied when it came to saying even the simplest phrases in English. I believed that the elementary education program was held all day. It was only at the end that I found out that elementary classes were held for only a couple of hours. The teachers had provided self-learning materials and the residents were working alone. I had been proud that we were providing this basic education and it turned out to be a sham. It was another of my disappointments.

One day with little notice, the Chino Board of Education decided it did not want to continue with CIW. We had to halt the elementary school programs because no other entity wanted to be responsible for the school. It took me almost a month to line up replacements through volunteer teachers from the surrounding communities. That was a frustrating situation.

I started to waiver. Perhaps I could never "fit in" to the Corrections system. Perhaps my attempts to "go by the rule book" were ill advised. Perhaps I should rely instead on my experience and capacity for creating solutions. But perhaps I am over-confident, relying upon previous successes in a much different setting. I felt confused and unsettled, trying to figure out the best approach to my new responsibilities.

Regular Hospital

The Regular Hospital was located in one wing of the Administration Building; it accommodated thirty patients. If more beds were needed, residents could be sent to a hospital in Chino or one of the other prison hospitals. The Hospital had lost its accreditation before I arrived. I was determined to learn what was needed to regain the accreditation. It was staffed by one Registered Nurse, two Licensed Vocational Nurses, the LVN residents in training and other residents who helped. The Registered Nurse looked to be seventy years old. She was a little sparrow-type, sharp-beaked lady who constantly chain smoked, dropping ashes over everything—very unprofessional.

We never had enough nursing help so we dared not speak crossly to anyone possessing those skills. Most of the nurses disliked the residents, and there were hostilities between the medical staff members and the residents. Many of the residents who came to the Hospital were malingerers. They were abusive, calling the nurses rude names and threatening them physically, screaming and spitting on them. The residents were permitted to write letters to the Governor so they wrote letters about abuses and the terrible conditions. Reading copies of these letters immediately raised my concern about what was going on in the Hospital. My investigation showed that the abuses and terrible conditions were exaggerations and that staff members were not out of line.

An inordinate number of residents had epilepsy, a much greater number than the average in the population outside. One resident had a particularly violent epileptic seizure and after she was brought to our Hospital, she unexpectedly died. This highlighted my concern about the medical treatment we had available. Our investigation revealed nothing out of the ordinary and that everything possible had been done to help that resident. That incident was disturbing to me, to the staff members and to the residents. One resident in particular, who was the lesbian partner of the deceased resident, became hysterical and demanded to go out of the prison to the funeral. She was a maximum custody resident and therefore could not leave the prison. She blamed me for this and whenever she saw me walking on the campus, she would shout and swear at me. Nothing would console her.

As related earlier, the Director of the Corrections Department, Jerry Enomoto himself, had temporarily headed CIW for about six months before he became Director of the Corrections Department in Sacramento so he knew about the failings of the place before I was appointed. Enomoto previously had been the Warden of the California Correctional Institution at Tehachapi for almost five years. Because the law says the Superintendent of CIW must be a woman, when Virginia Carlson resigned, he was assigned temporarily to CIW until a suitable candidate (me!) could be appointed. Enomoto knew he was only temporary. He'd had a whole career in the system. When I found all the problems in the Hospital and the food service and more, who had been the immediate previous Superintendent? Jerry Enomoto, the man who now was heading the Corrections Department. Enomoto had always been very kind to me. What was I going to do, complain to the media or to his superiors? Of course I decided against such a course of action.

In addition to medical treatment, the Hospital served also as a holding facility for a death row resident. The death sentence in California had been reinstated before I became Superintendent. The law requires when an inmate is sentenced to death, there must be a one-on-one Correctional Officer on duty on "death row" twenty-four hours, seven days per week, and specific living conditions must be established. CIW was not equipped for that. San Quentin prison has an entire wing of its high security building devoted to death row inmates. CIW had to locate a death row resident in its Hospital and arrange three shifts of one-on-one custody. When I was introduced to our "Death Row Maggie" I discovered that she was a harmless gray-haired little woman who stayed in her locked hospital room, knitting and watching television. Yes, she killed her husband after more than twenty years of enduring beatings, but it was a crime of passion; she wasn't dangerous to anyone. In the meantime, it took a Correctional Officer on every shift to maintain the required custody for Maggie.

On the Medical staff, George Rowland M.D. was an African American psychiatrist and the Chief Medical Officer. He was a jowly man about forty-five whose mouth turned down like an angry or annoyed person. Raised in a wealthy family, he was a dandy, seldom wearing the same suit or shirt twice. I learned later he was paid to be an expert witness in court cases. Doctor Rowland was one of the most negative people I had ever met; most of the residents disliked him. He delighted in putting people down, especially the residents who were his patients. Few of them ever wanted to consult with him about a problem.

I thought that Doctor Rowland was the wrong personality to be a psychiatrist in a prison setting. We became adversaries. He was convinced that I hated African Americans, which is absolutely not true. Everything I did or said, he would turn into a racial matter. It got to the point that I simply avoided him, and toward the end of my tenure, we did not speak to each other so I relied on his written reports to me. Because he was the only African American doctor in the entire Corrections system, I was powerless to encourage better performance from him.

Working for Rowland was another medical doctor, also a psychiatrist. He used to be a brilliant, dedicated man until he almost was killed in an auto accident that put him in a coma for an extended time. He had spells where he exhibited bizarre behavior, mumbling his words, getting extremely angry and not knowing who we were. Because he was a civil servant and also disabled, I did not know how to terminate him. He was intimidated by the residents who could bully him into dispensing drugs.

There is a demand for tranquilizers by residents in prison; they traffic in them, bartering for other goods. In the morning and afternoon pill lines where medications were dispensed through the pharmacy window, the nurses had to witness the residents actually taking the pills. Often, a nurse had to poke her fingers down residents' throats to ensure the pills were swallowed. The residents tried their best to conceal pills for future barter. It was an amusing "game" they enjoyed playing.

The third medical doctor was an independent contractor who had an ob-gyn practice in Chino. He had been hired to replace a civil service ob-gyn physician who made suggestive remarks while giving pelvic exams to the residents. Of course he denied it when he was confronted but he quickly resigned. Our Chino doctor was the only doctor we had on twenty-four hour call. I liked him very much and he helped me begin to understand the challenges we faced in the medical department and suggested many helpful strategies.

I was so apprehensive about the unacceptable situation in my hospital that I appealed to Enomoto personally. He had been supportive of my appointment. *There is going to be a terrible scandal or tragedy at CIW. I know nothing about running a hospital and I need technical help. We must get this Hospital running suitably before someone else dies.* Enomoto's administrative assistant, Norman Lewis, came to work at CIW for two months. A man in his thirties, he lived in the Pine Tree Motel and worked at CIW as a one-man task force to improve the Hospital. His report said that the conditions were appalling, that there was not enough equipment. He agreed that we shouldn't "blow the whistle" on Enomoto's failures. I knew privately that if I would say *This situation is inexcusable*, it would reflect negatively on my predecessor. We terminated the psychiatrist that was brain damaged. Lewis fired a couple of the nurses. He should have recommended to me that they be terminated and shown me how we could do it through civil service. The staff began wondering *Is Lewis running the Hospital or are you?*

Lewis obtained some unused equipment from other prisons. One of our Correctional Officers, Gwen Rowland, was a medical doctor, but not licensed in the United States. When I discovered this, I assigned her to the Hospital and asked her to work with Norman to determine what was necessary to achieve accreditation. She was an excellent addition to the Hospital staff. I felt much more confident about our medical services with Gwen and Norman as watch dogs in the Hospital. We didn't have any serious medical care problems there after they initiated needed improvements.

We had two dentists (civil servants); one of them was an alcoholic who spent his time sleeping on a cot in his office. There never was time to do any preventative dental work, as we did not have a dental technician. All we could do was respond to emergencies by drilling, filling or extracting. One resident wanted to be trained as a dental assistant, but the custody staff thought she could not be trusted with sharp instruments. The dental program was a failure. I did get rid of one of the dentists, forced him to retire and brought in another dentist who improved the situation.

We had Lab and X-Ray technicians but our equipment was so obsolete it was a disgrace. The residents should have been able to receive mammograms, but of course, there was no equipment for that.

At nearby Loma Linda Hospital, plastic surgeons were interning. Those young doctors were eager to come to CIW to practice. The residents wanted plastic surgery, the removal of tattoos and scars, the repair of ear lobes torn when earrings were pulled out during a fight and, of course, facelifts. I did not have problem with this, but before I came, two residents who had facelifts and eyelifts had problems. One woman could not close her eye as the procedure was such a failure. Another resident who had been a minor TV celebrity became psychotic about how her facelift looked. She kept bursting into my office with before and after pictures whenever she had a chance. I had to deal with her at least once a month trying to keep her from suing someone.

The State did not have to pay for plastic surgery services. The doctors came to practice for no charge. It made the residents happy. Then I discovered that residents could get pain killing drugs, so they clamored for surgery. I soon caught on to their "game" and became more involved with these procedures and put a stop to a great deal of the elective surgery. To accomplish this I insisted on looking personally at the resident and her case rather than looking only at her record.

Activities

Recreation. Sue Moore, our Recreation Director was a valued employee because of her positive attitude and her wide range of skills. About thirty, Sue was slim, attractive and smart. Like me, she came to CIW with high hopes of "making a difference" in some offenders' lives. Because we had so little funds for recreation, almost everything she requested for her programs was turned down for lack of maintenance or equipment. The tennis courts could not be used because there were no nets, racquets or balls. The recreation fields were overgrown and pocked with gopher holes. We sponsored a "kill the gophers" program so the fields could be leveled for a baseball diamond, which never was installed. I tried to implement an outdoor fitness program, but it was almost impossible to fit into other, high-priority schedules. The residents were required to be on their jobs or in classrooms from 8 A.M. to 5 P.M. unless they had a visitor or a formal, scheduled education class. Most residents had regular jobs. The ones who would not work were either "goldbricking" or had a doctor's excuse.

We tried to have special activities on holidays, there were a 4th of July picnic and a Labor Day picnic planned. When the gopher holes were filled I considered an outdoor barbecue for the entire campus where residents would be on the recreation field, and extra Correctional Officers would supervise the large group of residents and families. The Hispanic residents wanted to observe Cinco de Mayo (Fifth of May.) Being raised in Michigan I did not fully understand the importance of this day. Several staff members told me that celebrating Cinco de Mayo was just another excuse for the residents to have a party. However, after some research I did learn how much this date meant to the Mexican people. It was on May 5th 1862 that the Mexican Army defeated the French Expeditionary Forces at Puebla, near Mexico City. Learning of these historic events, I decided the date should be celebrated by showing the Mexican flag on the campus flagpole and serving Mexican cuisine for three meals that day. I took great satisfaction in being able to make those arrangements. And the Hispanic residents responded very happily.

Since its inception, the CIW facilities never were suitably maintained. In the early years, virtually all of the State's prison recreation funds went to the men's prisons. When Jerry Brown was elected Governor, the Corrections Department had to tighten its budget and the men's prisons lost about forty staff members. CIW did not suffer any personnel cuts because it already was down to the bare bones. To augment our "extras" such as books, clothing and a few items of recreational equipment I personally worked with outside groups. These activities came with a warning that it might embarrass the Governor due to the mandated budget constraints. We managed to form an alliance with Federation of Women's Clubs. Their members did donate clothing but our staff members had to search all items as the exact origin of the clothing was unknown. I persuaded several members to donate tennis racquets and balls and requested Scott to find enough money for two tennis nets. That cheered Sue considerably. She was such a helpful and loyal person. I tried to do everything in my power to make her work meaningful.

At some point in time prior to my appointment, a modest sized swimming pool had been built on one side of the campus. This had been accomplished at the request of the residents using their own funds. The pool had never really operated properly as the filtering equipment broke down when dirt clogged it. We could not afford to build a security fence or wind protective around it so every time there was a wind storm, the pool would be filled with dirt and leaves. This "white elephant" was open only one day during the time I was Superintendent. There weren't enough staff members to provide supervision of the pool so it became an attractive nuisance.

One afternoon, a group of residents became intoxicated on their home-made brew and jumped, fully clothed, into the pool. They did not bother to change into their donated swim suits. The Watch Commander, a balding, bow-legged little fellow ran from the Control Room to the pool and ordered the residents to get out. They just laughed and splashed him with water. He retreated to the Control Room and returned with a camera. *I'm taking your pictures for evidence*, he shouted. The residents responded by posing in silly and lewd postures. He then ran back to the Control Room and sounded the alarm for a campus-wide lockdown. This resulted in hundreds of residents running onto the campus from their jobs and classrooms. Some of these residents joined those already in the pool.

It was an absolute melee that took several hours to resolve. Ron Burke and the Watch Commander were summoned into my office to explain the circumstances. I pointed out there were many other ways to resolve the situation short of a disruptive lockdown. For example, several Correctional Officers could have been summoned to stand by the pool and not allow the offenders to get out until WE were ready. The all-campus alarm for lockdown was completely disruptive and should only be used in real emergencies. Ron was rebuked and the Watch Commander was given three days administrative leave without pay.

My job was keeping the residents in reasonable health and comfort and behind bars, for the allotted time, and not doing them harm. Where my predecessors got off the track was by starting programs and projects like the swimming pool without considering the future consequences. In order to gain better control of the prison, I had to order the pool "off limits." Although the residents had paid for the pool themselves, it was deactivated until future funds might become available for proper maintenance and construction of a security fence.

Part of the money residents earned was deposited into the Residents' Welfare Fund. Meanwhile, the State was getting its prison labor for a pittance. I thought if we paid prisoners the legal minimum wage for what they did, and expected them to pay for their room and board in prison, they would have more money left over and they would have respect for themselves. An idea ahead of its time! Prisons teach many inmates to become dependent on prison life. When they are released to society they have difficulty adjusting to the life outside. Many the residents did not need the constant vigilance that was provided. I was planning to institute an honor system or self-government for cooperative residents. The trouble makers would be placed into special intensive programs designed to watch them closely and prevent them from hurting each other or damaging the prison.

Movies and TV. Most of the films about women in prison and prison life have been seen on TV by the residents. Unfortunately these films serve to condition them to prison behavior, as portrayed in the movies. (If they had tin cups would they bang them on the bars?) My predecessor had selected some prison movies and horror movies, so residents had the opportunity to watch chainsaw massacre type of movies. Many residents were playing the game of being convicts. They enjoyed seeing crime and violence programs and were able to relate to them. If we did not show these in the day rooms, most residents had their own personal televisions in their rooms and could fill their minds with endless trash. I was hesitant to ban violent movies selected by the residents and paid for from the Inmates' Welfare Fund because of their First Amendment rights and pending court cases on this issue.

I did not try to censor programs except one time I interceded when the *Helter Skelter* movie about the Manson "Family" was to be shown. I contacted the attorney representing several of the Manson girls, and expressed concern that the movie might cause problems for the Manson girls incarcerated at CIW. Many of the residents had strong feelings about stabbing a pregnant woman; they were identifying with it. The Manson girls were making a good adjustment in the general population on the campus and I did not want any problems or having to isolate them again, so their attorney contacted the TV station and got the film removed from the schedule.

The Library. Housed in one of the classrooms, the library resembled one in an elementary school. The public donated books and the library program was supervised by a part-time volunteer, a housewife, who came in several days a week. Because we seldom had custody staff members assigned to the library, it was open only a few hours a day. As razors were sometimes found hidden in the bindings of some books, all had to be inspected before going on the shelves. On a positive note when the library was open it was used by many of the residents.

There were no newspapers in the library, so other than TV news, residents did not know what was happening in the world. I made a deal with the *Los Angeles Times* to donate their day-old papers. Again, I had to maintain the pretense that CIW had everything needed. I admit I took that instruction with a grain of salt.

As our law books were out of date, I squeezed funds from the budget to bring the law library up to date. One of the residents, Barbara, was an attorney who was trying not to be the "jailhouse" lawyer (a person who helps prison inmates research and file legal documents.) We did have several residents who appointed themselves to be jailhouse lawyers who worked with the residents preparing legal briefs and appeals for them. One of these was Florence who was moved from working as assistant secretary in the Superintendent's office. The other residents mostly left her alone. She had little to do all day except fire off letters and write proposals to present to the prison administration.

Gardening. CIW had fruit trees, but these had to be cut down because residents stole the fruit and combining fruit with bread pellets made "hooch" with it. In another area, we wanted to create vegetable gardens because there were not enough fresh vegetables, and many of the residents wanted to garden. I could relate to that and believed a gardening program would be something I could enjoy doing with the residents. The Southern California climate is perfect for year-around gardening so not taking advantage of that would have been regrettable. Growing our own fresh vegetables would have been a positive undertaking. We had no tractors or plows or farm implements, but we were in the process of getting some used equipment. Our site was 120 acres. We had a full time gardener who worked in the greenhouse cultivating special plants for the interiors of the buildings. Some residents enjoyed working with the gardener to plan the crops we would plant in the spring of 1976. Meanwhile, they concentrated on planting flower seeds outside the cottages and around the various buildings. We had to keep a look-out for a certain psychotic resident who enjoyed trampling down the flowers.

Religious Observance. CIW had three civil service religious leaders, Catholic, Protestant and Jewish. There was no chapel because the California Legislature would not fund a chapel for CIW. Although we lobbied and wrote letters, CIW was the only prison in the State without a church—a nondenominational place of worship. There was no location to have religious meetings other than in the classrooms.

The rabbi came weekly to conduct services but the Jewish residents did not want his ministrations because he was an Orthodox Jew. At that time, the Jewish residents were either Conservative or Reform Jews. I was the only Superintendent they ever had that understood the difference between Orthodox, Conservative and Reform Judaism. When I suggested to the rabbi that he was not serving the needs of the residents he was persuaded to modify his program. The Jewish residents were pleased that I had interceded in their behalf. At Passover; I was invited to attend the special dinner we provided for them. I had to decline the residents' request that the Jewish men housed at CIM in Chino be invited to the dinner. Such an event would have been fodder for the media.

The Catholic priest held a service every Sunday. The priest disliked having to serve at CIW as he feared the residents. All was going well however until a small group of residents who practiced Satanism broke into the classroom closet where the priest kept the sacred materials for the Catholic service. Pins were stuck in his idols, the candlesticks were bent and the supplies were ruined. It took a long time for him to get over the sacrilege of the Satanists. He was so shaken that for two weeks, we had to find a substitute priest. The Satanists faded away so none of the culprits was ever identified and punished.

The Protestant minister came and went quietly so I did not learn much about his contribution to the religious program.

Vocational Programs

There was no history of programs that had been tried at CIW. I would get an idea about a new program to try but the staff members would tell me it would not work. Against prevailing opinion, I initiated a program where residents could volunteer for certain jobs and be assigned to a cottage with others in the same job. For example, all the residents who worked in the kitchen could live in a specific cottage because they had to arise early to start breakfast. Housing residents together who had common traits, or classes or interests worked well in establishing relatively stress-free living conditions in the cottages. The plan also helped the Correctional Counselors hold their group therapy sessions, because the commonalities of the residents led to easier problem-solving in a group atmosphere.

After sentencing, residents were classified into work programs. There were various job openings all the time. Residents worked in the kitchen at the Village Cafeteria, in the education building, in the greenhouse, in the library and a few worked as helpers in the hospital. "Pots & Pans" in the kitchen was a punishment. If the staff members did not like a resident they would have her cleaning pots and pans for a couple of years. On occasion, I would receive a plaintive note from a resident: *Help! I've been on pots and pans for almost two years and have exhausted all remedies.* I would investigate and have her transferred. Four residents cooked and served in the Employee Snack Bar where staff members dined. Of course that is where staff members talk about happenings in the prison, so immediately news, gossip and rumors got back to the campus. There could be no secrets at CIW.

Food Service Training. Residents counted themselves lucky to be assigned to cooking in the Village Cafeteria. It was a preferential job saved for the best behaved residents. It was a "natural" job for most women, although learning to cook for large numbers was a new experience. Cookbooks from military mess halls were used and the kitchen was the rare place where necessary equipment was available. I enjoyed touring the kitchen, watching residents filling the huge vats with hearty soups and stews.

After Connie took leave of absence, I created a new Food Service Training Program because of the rumbling about the terrible food. I assigned a staff member to attend every meal we served and sample it and give me a written report. These reports were always positive. Often I would get after the fact notes from residents that the food was "garbage." I had to rely on the staff meal reporting and my own weekly lunches at the Village Cafeteria. I never announced when I was coming. The food was better than I ever had at summer camp so I did not over-react. When I looked at some military facilities and studied their food service practices I realized that we were doing a fairly good job feeding residents on a budget of $3.00 per day per person for three meals.

The Food Service Training Program was established in cooperation with Chaffee College. It was an innovative program whereby residents could earn college credits and certificates in food preparation. There was a similar program working at another prison, so I found the technical person, Larry David, who designed that program. I used my influence to have him transferred to CIW to run the Food Service and the new Training Program. One of the enjoyable classroom subjects was food garnishing, how to make radish roses, carrot pinwheels and more. Suddenly artistry in the Village Cafeteria began to bloom with fantastically garnished slices of bologna—still bologna but it greatly helped the morale.

CIW offered Mexican food, tacos and enchiladas a couple times a week. Soul food was served about once a week consisting of ham hocks, black-eyed peas and greens. Most residents accustomed to this fare enjoyed it without complaints. When pork was served some other kind of protein was available to accommodate the Jewish residents and those other residents who would not eat pork. Keeping a kosher kitchen was not an option.

Breakfast was a common menu in all the dining rooms. Lunch and dinner were three different menus in the three dining rooms. Residents could eat in the dining room that appealed to them. One was devoted to a salad bar, the second offered meat and potato items while the third dining room served soups and sandwiches. It was hard to know each day which residents would eat where. Residents could not have more than one entrée—meat, poultry, eggs or fish—but they never went hungry. Residents could have as much salad, soup and bread as they wanted. The extensive luncheon salad bar was established to appease residents who wanted to lose weight.

Larry was learning who was going to eat what so he could plan the food and control the budget. But the residents tried to go from one dining room to another eating multiple meals and that was not in the budget. This was controlled by a new procedure. After a resident entered a dining room she had to remain there until the meal was over, and meals would be over simultaneously in all three dining rooms. Residents tried to keep coming and going though, so it was difficult to monitor the situation.

After I resigned, the Food Service Training Program was abandoned, Larry David was reassigned and the food service reverted to its previous level. So much for perceived progress!

Commercial Sewing. CIW had a large commercial sewing factory where residents sewed garments for hospitals and men's prisons. Residents also made jackets and fluorescent clothing for highway workers and for many other State uses. They were paid 6¢ an hour deposited into their prison bank accounts. Many of the skills residents were learning and the equipment they used were obsolete, so they could not readily translate their experience into a real-world job. In spite of that, residents assigned to the sewing factory enjoyed the work and the satisfaction of completing a garment.

Silk Screen Program. We established a silk screen training program that was enjoyed by the more artistic residents. They made posters, T-shirts and small items to be sold in the Visiting Room. There was a sizable waiting list of residents wanting to participate in the training. Our budget for supplies was small so I managed to obtain materials that were donated by several private silkscreen firms in town. One of the residents called Grace was an African American woman with a big Afro hair style. She was the president of the Resident Council and also the editor of the residents' Newspaper. As the leader of the resident group, she was a cool lady, quite cooperative. Grace had aspirations of learning the printing business. We assigned her to the new silk screen program where she became adept and created many artistic projects and posters that were widely admired. One day I asked her *Grace, why do you always wear a stocking cap?* She thought a moment. *Well Ms. Carey, when I go on campus with just my Fro,* grackles (noisy black birds) *land on my head and poop on me. They think my Fro is a nest! The stockin' cap keeps the poop off me.* It was hard to conceal my amusement.

Cosmetology. Hair styling is one of the popular programs in a women's prison. Our Cosmetology school was well equipped and had an impressive African American woman, Cecelia Lawson, as the teacher. She was a civil service employee, a licensed cosmetologist and was custody-trained. This was an excellent background for working with difficult residents. In Cosmetology, residents have access to razors and scissors and other potential weapons. Residents frequently "forgot" to lockup the razors and scissors, but Cecelia was on top of monitoring the inventory and accounting for everything.

A number of the really dangerous or disruptive African American residents were assigned into Cosmetology whether or not they wanted to be beauticians, because Cecelia had wonderful ways of keeping them calm and focused. Many residents passed the required courses to obtain a State Cosmetology license. If they were minimum custody residents or nearing their parole date, they were escorted out of the prison to take the State examination for their licenses. The maximum security residents never went outside of CIW other than for a medical emergency. Those residents could be re-classified to minimum or medium security as their parole dates approached.

The Cosmetology students invited me to have my hair styled and many of the female staff members took advantage of that. But I was hesitant about lying with my neck on the shampoo bowl and my throat potentially exposed to a razor. One day I noticed in the local newspaper that the Broadway department store was advertising a wig sale. When a used wig was turned in, a discount was given on a new one. Aha! I drove into Los Angeles to the Broadway store and explained to the Manager what we wanted. I was given a large plastic bag of used wigs and I signed a paper promising these would not be worn by anyone. Some of the wigs were dreadful, but the residents cleaned them first and had fun practicing on them. After they became adept in handling wigs I let the residents clean and style two of my wigs. They styled them into Afros. I knew they meant well and were trying to please me.

Audio-Visual Workshop. A successful one-time program was an Audio-Visual Workshop. Nancy Graham, an independent TV producer from San Francisco, obtained a grant to film a documentary at CIW. Nancy was a talented young woman who got along well with the residents. In addition to being attractive, Nancy was exceptionally intelligent and provided me with many valued insightful comments about CIW life. She conducted a very innovative training program and helped the residents make a film comprised primarily of thirty-second television spots that were pieced together with narration. In the spots, various individual residents talked against drugs and about prison life. I believe that film still is available at CIW.

Secretarial Training. International Business Machines (IBM) donated about thirty typewriters and a comprehensive secretarial training program was proposed. When a teacher could not be found, we looked for volunteers without success. I yearned to teach the course myself, but with all I had on my plate that was completely impractical. Sadly, the typewriters remained in an empty classroom during my time as Superintendent. Every time I passed that classroom I would feel a grinding sensation in my stomach from the frustration of not being able to move forward with this program.

Outside Groups

We had groups that came into CIW—Alcoholics Anonymous, the religious leaders and several others. The Alcoholics Anonymous group liked to do social self-help, and in a prison they have a captive group of residents. Unfortunately we did not have a much needed narcotics rehab group. One problem is that some narcotics groups want to work in the prison for the wrong reasons, so those people must be extensively checked out before being permitted to work inside the walls. Also, the California Rehabilitation Center located in Corona, attracted most of the legitimate narcotics rehab volunteers.

One of our groups, Friends from Outside, was headed by a talented woman named Mary. She and her group met frequently with residents and did meaningful social work. I did not know that Mary was a Roman Catholic nun until I overheard someone calling her Sister. The residents liked and trusted her so she obtained positive results with some of the most difficult residents.

The Riverside-San Bernardino Chapter of the California National Organization for Women (NOW) worked with members of the Circle's Edge, a feminist organization at the prison. The group discusses many things: those rehabilitative jobs that do not prepare a woman to support herself when released, inadequate medical care and mothers' concerns for their children. The NOW women provided small money for an emergency release fund to sponsor Circle's Edge members who might need to go home on furlough in case of a family crises.

Parole Board

The Chair of the CIW Parole Board, Joann West, was an appointee of former Governor Ronald Reagan. The staff members prepared me by saying that Mrs. West was an unreasonable, difficult person. They said that she prevented paroles without just cause for residents who clearly had been rehabilitated. To familiarize myself with the Parole Board process, I sat in on a couple of their meetings, held in a room across from my office three days a week.

I made a determined effort to get to know and understand Mrs. West. I discovered that she was smart, charming and conscientious and displayed none of the traits suggested by the staff. We became good friends. At one point, she became somewhat preoccupied with thoughts of angels on earth by reading a number of "angel" books. She told me one day that she believed I was an angel, and did I know that? Actually, I had been asked that over the past years by several unrelated people. Something in my personality perhaps had prompted those assumptions. Of course, if I really was an angel on earth, I could have singlehandedly solved the numerous problems at CIW. The suggestion made me smile.

Sometimes a resident would confess to a crime and implicate other people, whereas she previously had maintained innocence. After several years of confinement a resident might say, *Yes, I did that and so-and-so was involved.* Then the matter would be referred to the local police for follow-up investigation. Once, when I was an observer, a resident confessed to the Parole Board that she was guilty and was sorry. The Parole Board's unwritten rule was that until a resident confessed to being guilty and apologized, she would not be released. That was in the days of California's indeterminate sentence. Whether or not that particular resident was guilty, I do not know. I discussed this with Mrs. West, who notified the court to change the resident's records to document a guilty plea.

Several times I appealed to the Board to re-review a specific resident's file because I believed the resident was ready to be released. Frequently the Board agreed that my advice had merit and my recommendations were followed. It felt good to cut the red tape and prevail over bureaucracy. The word got around the campus that the Superintendent would go to bat for a deserving resident. My popularity with the residents grew and toward the end of the year the staff members reported that most of the residents felt quite positively toward me. I could tell the difference in the climate on the campus. As I walked about, residents would come up to talk or to call out a friendly greeting and wave.

There were two residents who were friends before their conviction. Their sentences were Life Without Possibility of Parole. They were the only residents at CIW with that sentence at that time. They were in their early twenties, young mothers with small children. Their crime? They were on a "double date" with their husbands and stopped in a local bar in the wee hours. Their husbands befriended the bar maid and the men and the barmaid made a plan to take the money from the cash register and claim the bar was robbed. The men, their wives and the barmaid got in the men's car and drove to a wooded area. The men got out with the barmaid while the wives waited in the car. The men then shot the barmaid to death and the four of them drove home. I do not know the details of how they were caught or tried in court.

Before being appointed as Superintendent of CIW, I had not thought much about the death penalty. Although I believed the sentence pronounced upon Maggie in death row was inappropriate, I began to be a strong supporter of the death penalty for heinous crimes. This is because an alternative penalty of Life Without Possibility of Parole is difficult for all concerned. What would keep a resident with such a sentence from harming a staff member or another resident? What would be a way to motivate such a resident to exhibit good behavior? After interviewing those two residents serving Life Without Possibility of Parole, I told them that if they would be on their best behavior, I would ask the Governor to commute their sentences after they had served at least ten years. I am sorry I left CIW before I could do that for them.

Conjugal Visits

A suite of apartments upstairs over my office had housed the Superintendent years ago. These apartments had then been made into Family Visiting Units. When I arrived at CIW, the apartments looked like a skid row hotel. I promoted Shirley, my secretary, to Manager of Special Projects to bring these units up to acceptable living standards. She was to redecorate and buy newer ranges and refrigerators. She found some good used furniture and window coverings and stocked the kitchens with household goods. Instead of broken down furniture and mattresses on the floor, we provided a pleasant, clean place for residents to visit with their families. Family visits were an important motivator. More than seventy-five percent of residents had children under age eighteen. During staff meetings the patter of little feet running up and down and the screaming of children at play overhead became a nuisance that we were content to ignore.

A married resident who was not maximum security could be entitled to a conjugal visit on a weekend. She would produce a marriage license but usually the marriage was in her records and already had been verified by the court. The visit would start Friday night and the resident would go back to her room Sunday night. The families brought food and cooked in the apartments. The security over the Family Visiting Units was not very strict. The in-coming food baskets were searched for drugs and contraband but many already prepared food items could only be probed so far. Residents were required to come downstairs every six hours (yes, twenty-four hours a day) and be counted with the rest of the prison's inmates, so the visiting situation was monitored somewhat.

Unmarried residents were permitted to have visits from their boyfriends only in the Residents' Visiting Room, which was a small accommodation for over seven hundred residents. However, they could schedule a visit in the Family Visiting Unit with relatives and children. Although the courts recognize common law marriage, the prison system had different rules. For instance, the courts ruled that sex acts between consenting unmarried adults in California is not illegal, but in prison that is a felony. At the time I was appointed, the Corrections Department was considering staying out of the prisoners' personal lives, and if they wanted to get married, let them. But it did not occur to the Department that this could refer to a female prisoner marrying a male prisoner. That would entail the transportation of inmates between prisons, a situation that was unanticipated.

One of our resident groups was WHIP (Wives and Husbands in Prison.) WHIP also had a chapter at each California men's prison. I arranged for two of our WHIP members to be transported to the California Correctional Institution at Tehachapi to have a conjugal visit with their husbands who were imprisoned there. That worked so well I decided to help a third resident by arranging her marriage to a man who then was in prison at Tehachapi. They had children together but had never legally married. This type of marriage occurrence had never happened in the whole history of the California prison system. I prearranged through the Tehachapi Warden for one of his officials who had business at CIW to bring the prospective groom with him. We organized the ceremony with the Protestant minister, held a small wedding reception with a decorated cake, decked out the Family Visiting Unit as a honeymoon suite and the newlyweds enjoyed a conjugal visit. The story was in many California newspapers. For me, that wedding was one of the kindest things I was able to accomplish. I did not track their matrimonial history after the event but I like to think their union has survived.

The staff members planned parties with each cottage. Initially, I thought parties were a good idea. The residents would decorate their cottages and have special food and some kind of a festive activity like card games or contests. They were generally enjoyable events at which residents would have an afternoon off or a free evening although under the supervision of staff members. Prior to the coming Christmas season, I learned the residents' idea of a party would be an occasion where families would come into the prison bringing a wide array of prepared food and gifts. The party would not be in the Visitors' Room as I assumed, but would be held in the cottage with the children and a long list of relatives.

Of course, along with the food, sharp instruments and narcotics were smuggled in. The narcotics were often disguised as "bath salts." One woman, in her forties brought along her infant during a visit with her nineteen year old daughter. In searching the diaper a narcotics kit was found, and the woman was arrested. She soon became a resident along with her daughter. With these types of challenges and distractions to our security measures, I appointed a task force to plan ways to reduce risks while still permitting residents to participate in reasonable visitation activities. Changing the rules relating to the scope of these parties became the cause of an unanticipated major disturbance within CIW at the end of December.

The CIW Routine

I vacated the Pine Tree motel in May and moved into our newly-purchased house near Riverside. It was U-shaped, with a patio inside of the U. The house was on a gravel road and was surrounded by several acres of grassland with many trees. It was isolated and private. I bought a king bed and a few household items and waited eagerly for Bill's arrival from Michigan with the furniture. On the appointed day, I kept glancing out of the window and suddenly, there he was, driving up to the front door. He sprang out of the car and met me at the door with a handful of flowers, slightly wilted but lovely. After a lingering embrace, I was eager to give him a tour of the property. I had purchased the house without his input, and was relieved that he loved it. Overlooking the hazards of my new position, I had not considered the danger of living in relative isolation. I even had listed our address and phone number in the telephone directory! That was naïve, to say the least. At my request, Bill took several months to settle us in the house before he looked for employment.

On a typical day, I would arrive at CIW about 7:30 A.M. as the Watch was changing. The Watch Commander would assemble the day staff members in the Visiting Room and read aloud the log that was a report of happenings during the previous eight hours. After the reading I would go to my office with a cup of coffee and meet with Ron Burke to discuss custody problems from the previous night and what the new day could bring. For example, someone would be caught in a lesbian situation in someone else's room and that is a felony, or someone had gotten into a fight. With only two Correctional Officers in each cottage with one hundred fifty rooms; it was fairly easy for residents to come and go, steal things and make trouble. I enjoyed working with Ron and depended upon him to help me learn the ropes. But it was hard to dismiss the feeling I had that Ron was trying to compete with me for my job.

Next, I would meet with AllenBrown to discuss the schedule for visitors that day and to get feedback from the Correctional Counselors regarding any residents who needed special attention. AllenBrown was always cheerful, joking. His sunny disposition brightened my mornings. Other typical meetings included meeting daily with the physicians and the head of the two Hospitals (regular care and psychiatric care) and be briefed on what treatments and surgeries would occur. The final decision was up to the Chief Medical Officer concerning who got what treatment or surgery. On a regular basis I met with union groups, the Teamsters, the California State Employees and two or three other groups. Then there was an Employees' Council that consisted of one representative from each department: the nurses, the kitchen workers, the landscapers and so on. I also met weekly with the Residents' Council.

Once a week I had a staff meeting in the conference room with all the key people I've described, to update one another and me. At least weekly I had visitors from the Corrections Department, or a visitor that I would tour and entertain. The Superintendent's job is partially public relations so we entertained many outside people who wanted to learn what is going on inside the prison. I looked forward to showing our programs and operations to outsiders. That was a task that called upon some of my best qualities. We could use all the outside good-will that could be mustered.

I invited judges to come to CIW to see their sentencing carried out. One judge accepted and came with his secretary. I toured them around the campus and hosted them for lunch in the Village Cafeteria. It was a revelation for the judge. *Don't you have a substance abuse program at CIW? I thought you had a rehab program here.* I was quick to point out that persons convicted of a drug offense were sent to the nearby Corona facility. We did the best we could for those residents who had a drug problems but were sent to CIW for a non drug related crime.

I had promoted Shirley from secretary to Manager of Special Projects because she was a capable person, but acted as though she was in charge of CIW. I suppose it was because she had worked there a long time and knew what the secrets were. I respected her knowledge, but I never was convinced of her loyalty to me. I had the feeling that she was trying to compete with me at every turn. During the first few weeks I was at CIW, Shirley arranged a get-together at her house one evening, inviting me and the female Correctional Counselors. My recollection is that these women crowded around me saying in urgent voices, *You've got to do this ... you've got to do that ...* I was bothered by that because I did not feel they were in a position to dictate my actions. I wanted their in-put but resented being told that I had to do certain things. I knew they meant well, but the meeting just confirmed my impression that Shirley and her minions were trying to pull my strings.

Shirley's replacement, Beverly Morgan, had been a clerk in the Records Office before being promoted to Superintendent's secretary. She was twenty-five, dark eyed, very attractive, with a radiant personality and excellent skills. I had noticed her and personally selected her for promotion because she was a diligent worker and was smart and cooperative. It was a pleasure to have Beverly in my corner because she was unstintingly loyal and knew her way around the daily obstacles. We liked each other immediately and worked together with ease. We became very close friends.

Because I expected to be the Superintendent for the future, I was forming strategic plans. The budget was inherited from my predecessor so I had to operate on that budget until the end of 1975. One of my business strengths is forward planning rather than minute-to-minute implementation. I never really worried about that because the Corrections Department said they had given me the right people to get the job done. I figured that was the way things were everywhere in the system. The staff members delighted in "teaching" the new Superintendent. I was eager to learn and took it all in but balked if they assumed a superior role.

Not only was I bogged down in making decisions without sufficient information, but my staff members told me what my role was, that I wasn't to do this or I shouldn't do that. I learned too late that the Deputy Superintendent, Ron Burke, had been instructed by our boss, Walt Cooper, to run CIW secretly and that I was to be just the figurehead. Walt Cooper effectively prevented me from doing the job I was appointed to do. Because the law requires the Superintendent to be a woman, the Corrections Department set it up for their appointee to be virtually powerless, and the men were told to run the prison behind her back. I had two male Deputy Superintendents and they had the pipeline to and from the "top brass" in the Corrections Department, who were men. I did not suspect that I was a figurehead and did not know that my boss was communicating with the Deputy Superintendents almost every day. I did wonder why my boss seldom phoned me or spoke to me. I assumed that was because I was doing a satisfactory job. **This situation was the root of my powerlessness in taking charge of the problems at CIW.**

I wondered how the other Wardens did their jobs so readily. When I visited other prisons, there would be the Warden with a clean desk, no meetings on his calendar. I would say *How do you do that? I'm working my ass off down there without a day off. I'm doing almost every damn job in the place because there is not enough staff authorized.* How could these men manage their prisons so well and I could not manage mine effectively? Their methods eluded me. **How could I have known that I had intentionally been set up to have no real authority?**

One of the most difficult challenges imposed on CIW was being required to implement the <u>entire</u> Affirmative Action Program for all the State prisons at our one prison. We were not permitted to hire the people needed for a certain job unless they were a specified ethnicity or a specified sex. We could scarcely staff the place and had to take almost anyone who was a warm body who happened to be a Hispanic or an African American female. (I never was able to recruit an African American or Hispanic female Boiler Operator or Fire Chief.) I just figured this was a rigid system, and everyone else was making it work. There must be something I was lacking. Women usually assume that when things go wrong, it must be their fault. **It never occurred to me that incompetence of my superiors might be the subtle reason.**

The Corrections Department was trying to make its Affirmative Action Program look good on paper. When I was appointed, the Corrections Department transferred most of the top female staff members that could have helped to run CIW and assigned them to other prisons, leaving me with few experienced senior women. Even if the situation exploded, the myth is that women do not riot; they just cry and act-out. Actually, at that time CIW had more assault with deadly weapons convictions and first degree murderers than were in Folsom, the toughest of the California prisons. The public would be amazed at the number of heavy-duty residents at CIW. We managed to keep those women cool. We could not afford to have anything go wrong because we did not have the facilities to deal with certain situations. So the prison management at CIW got into the habit of placating, and they placated for years until I arrived. My major mistake was thinking that the administration, not the residents, was running the prison.

Implementing the Affirmative Action Program became such a focal point that I requested a visit from Carrie Johnson, Director of Affirmative Action for the Corrections Department. Carrie was a very attractive African American, about thirty-five. Carrie had red hair and green eyes. Her long fingernails flashed shiny red polish. She was dressed like a model. I do not know what her background and training were but she oozed self-confidence. I confided my concerns about being able to implement all the demands of Affirmative Action while managing CIW efficiently. I told her I didn't want to be terminated by the Department over such an unrealistic task. Carrie just laughed and putting her hand on my shoulder uttered the most unforgettable sentence I heard during my year in the prison. *Don't worry about a thing, Brook, because you and I are golden!* I wanted to be valued because I was a smart, effective leader, not just because I was a female. Carrie was not very helpful in guiding me about the Program. I was left to my own devices.

A major difficulty was that CIW had to be all things to the residents because at this time there was only one California woman's prison and it had to meet every kind of requirement. (In 2008 there are four.) For example, why isn't there a college program at Soledad? The Warden could say if residents want to go to college, let them transfer down to CIM that has a college program. Or why doesn't every men's prison have a psychiatric unit? They can be sent to the California Medical Center for treatment. There usually is a place for every type of situation in the men's prison system. Male inmates are put on the prison bus, and the bus shuttles between the men's prisons, and if a man needs a certain program, he is bused to a certain prison. That was called "bus therapy." With women inmates, CIW was alone in attempting to meet all their reasonable needs. We were vulnerable to every complaint about why we did not have a drug program, or why we did not offer this or that. I found myself more and more in a defensive mode while trying to meet every realistic demand.

Bill was my valued "kitchen cabinet" advisor. I talked with him about my challenges, and coming from the military, he understood the problems. His experience as an executive at General Motors had further groomed him in working with bureaucracy. But staff members liked to think *You're married to a retired Army officer and he is in charge* so I did not mention him as a source of some of my ideas and solutions. I wanted to develop solutions on my own that would enhance my learning curve. However, Bill did give me a number of excellent suggestions. One of these, regarding isolation and special treatment of the trouble makers was just about to be implemented when events happened to change priorities.

Bill also had a knack for identifying fixable problems. For example, he suggested that a new type of barbed wire, concertina wire, be installed instead of barbed wire on top of the chain link perimeter fence to discourage escapes. I told Scott that CIW should be using this new kind of barbed wire to prevent residents from escaping. I was learning the ropes. Scott asserted *Concertina wire is not in the budget. You can't have that.* I replied forcefully *I know there isn't money in the budget. Get it anyway, damn it!* So Scott somehow obtained a supply of wire. It was installed on top of the perimeter fence and the rusty, broken barbed wire was removed. The new wire was such an effective barrier that escapes over the fence were eliminated. Although no one succeeded in climbing over the wire, several tried and became cut by its razor-sharp design. One resident who did try but failed to climb over the concertina wire filed a law suit against me for her cuts and damages!

I also was being sued by Mary Brunner, Charles Manson's common law wife, for keeping her in a locked room at night. I spoke to Harold Williams about the law suits and asked for guidance. The Wardens of the men's prisons had banded together for mutual financial protection against personal lawsuits against them. *What about me?* I wondered. *You're on your own* Harold Williams told me. I replied *You mean an inmate can sue me personally for any reason and the Corrections Department doesn't do anything to help me? That's right*, he said calmly. I resolved to look into buying personal liability insurance protection. Another item added to my 'to do' list that never came to the top of pile.

Another difficulty I encountered was the established chain of command. My colleagues were not business people, so I had to help them supervise all of their subordinates. I was aiming for a maximum of seven people to report directly to me. At first I had fourteen people reporting to me just to stay updated. In a prison important events happen quickly every day. There was not any way to rely on written reports because there were only two secretaries who could transcribe. I did not want to use residents as secretaries because we lose control when they know too much about what is going on within the system.

I concluded that there was a small nucleus of about fifty residents keeping CIW in an uproar. These fifty residents were taking about ninety percent of staff time. They would make "hooch," pick fights, steal from other residents and deal in contraband. Those fifty residents received an inordinate amount of 115s for dozens of infractions that kept the staff members busy investigating and having hearings. It was difficult to get on with positive business. The solutions to many of these problems are obvious when looking back on them. As the Superintendent, the environment of the prison was so out of the ordinary and so removed from my range of experience that it affected my ability to think clearly and solve problems effectively.

When the public thinks about prisons, they picture hardened criminals locked in small cells. At CIW, even though there were maximum security residents, it basically was a minimum security facility. Only very few residents were locked in their rooms during the day. Residents went to jobs, classrooms, the Library, the Hospital, and many lounged about the campus. This contributed to giving the trouble makers free rein to make their mischief. The staff members spent most of their time reacting to events. We could not catch up with the priorities to enable us to be proactive.

Relating with Residents

Women in prison are considerably different from men concerning the type of criminality. Men are more likely to commit violent crimes and women more prone to commit property crimes. Women are more likely to be convicted and incarcerated for minor offenses. Studies show that women tend to commit crimes of survival to earn money and escape cruel physical relationships. The reality for many women is a world of drugs, abusive men, no employment and no social support for themselves and their children. For many, the structured atmosphere at CIW offered a welcome situation. Many residents liked the environment so well that they were reluctant to leave when paroled. In effect, the prison system is designed to deal with the criminality of men. In California, the system was not equipped to handle women's problems that bring them to prison and the problems they deal with while incarcerated. With the emphasis on security and population management and the lack of focus on treatment and programs, prisons are poorly equipped to deal with the failure of society's misfits.

Family structures become established among women in prison. This does not necessarily mean homosexual relationships but rather groups of women join together for support, comradeship and friendship. Some women play mother or sister roles, and indeed some strong, resourceful women play the father role. Many women serving long sentences lose their outside connections which makes the inside family connections even more valued. Visitors to women's prisons tend to be caretakers of residents' children and female family members rather than male partners.

Interaction between experienced staff members and residents generally is positive. The daily routines are comfortable and predictable: wake up, head count, breakfast, work/school, lunch, head count, work/school, dinner, head count, activity, lights-out, head count. Residents learn that treating staff members with respect earns respect in return. During my time as the Superintendent, I seldom heard a complaint about staff members' inappropriate behavior. Surprisingly, such behavior appeared to be the norm in the men's prisons. I do not believe that residents at CIW had fears of being molested, beaten or mistreated in any way during my tenure. I'm sure I would have known about any such situation. I encountered nothing at CIW that even remotely resembled the women's prison films Hollywood produced.

I became acquainted with a number of residents to know their names and understand their attitudes and actions. I seldom talked to residents about their cases. Discussing cases was not advised. Usually, after residents talk about their cases—many protesting their innocence—they would want to argue their beliefs with me about the issue. It was best to assume the residents were guilty of the crimes of which they were convicted and proceed on that supposition. There were not enough staff members to deal with residents individually. All we could do was to react to what they did on the scene. For example, if residents were threatening someone or acting in a violent manner, we handled that directly. Or we might study their case history and try to determine a future strategy for them. But after residents were going to school or to their jobs and not causing trouble there was not time to wonder why they were in CIW.

The following are my recollections of several of the most memorable residents I met during my year at CIW.

BUBBLE-UP: She came up to me in the center of the campus during my first day on the job. Dressed in man's clothing and a fedora, she sidled up and whispered in a hoarse voice *My name is Bubble-Up!* What an amusing name, I thought. (I did not know that Bubble-Up was a soft drink favored by Californians.) She continued with small talk, gesturing broadly, for several minutes. Then she abruptly turned and walked away. I was puzzled by that exchange because I had been warned that residents seldom do anything without an ulterior motive. Captain Madge told me later that Bubble-Up had announced to the resident population that she had confronted the new Superintendent and told the Superintendent just how she wanted matters to be managed from now on. That was my first introduction to residents' "games." I don't remember seeing Bubble-Up around on the campus after that. Perhaps she was hiding from me.

BETTY LOU: As the State's oldest female inmate in 1975 at seventy-six, Betty Lou had entered CIW in 1935 after killing her landlady during an argument. She had many friends among the residents who visited her in the Hospital where we housed her. She had a sunny personality and enjoyed hearing jokes. She heard the Corrections Department was trying to set up a program for residents at CIW to have their small children and babies with them. Betty Lou told me that she was practicing, in her mind, the "Granny skills" and looking forward to being a volunteer baby sitter in the new program. Although she was somewhat fragile, she delighted in her daily job folding sheets. Do-gooders kept trying to have her paroled, but she did not want to leave. CIW was home to her. I liked Betty Lou and was happy to try to help her stay at CIW. Her family was long-gone and I believed she was too old to adjust to life alone on the outside.

ANNA: At twenty-eight, Anna was an African American, beautiful enough to be a model. Along with Florence, she had been working in the Superintendent's office as assistant secretary to Shirley. She came from a wealthy family in Los Angeles. She and her husband had master's degrees in pharmacology. They worked together in a pharmacy and surreptitiously were dispensing drugs without prescriptions before they were arrested and incarcerated. When Anna was apprehended, her family had high political connections with the Democratic Party and was trying to pull strings to keep her out of prison. When this became known, Anna was sent to CIW to demonstrate to her family that they could not exert influence. Anna was a person who normally would have been put on parole; she was soft voiced and gentle, not at all a hardened criminal type.

Anna continued to act as if she was my secretary, even after she was transferred out of the Administration Building to be secretary in the Education Department. She'd come tripping up to me on campus, *Hello, Mrs. Carey, how's everything going? I miss you.* She was one of the highly-respected residents in the prison, she wasn't in on any of the subterfuge; she kept her distance from trouble makers.

Anna was President of the WHIP organization—Wives and Husbands in Prison. I arranged to take her to Tehachapi to have a conjugal visit with her husband. I did not know that he was Caucasian until we arrived. None of the Tehachapi prison officials knew that his wife was African American and we arranged the visit with no thoughts of racism. When I arrived with an African American woman to have a conjugal visit with a Caucasian man there was backlash from a few of the prisoners and staff members. Remember, this was the 1970s and intolerance was the status quo. On the drive back to CIW, Anna was appreciative about the visit. She reminded me that her parole date was coming soon and we discussed her plan to rent an apartment in the city of Tehachapi and seek employment there to be near her husband. I liked Anna very much and believed she had paid for her offense. When I offered to write a letter of reference for her, she had tears to her eyes.

FLORENCE: The resident who took me on my first tour of CIW was about forty-three, attractive, plump. Always carefully made-up and dressed in expensive clothing, Florence looked like a high-society matron. I learned that her ex-husband was a doctor, so her appearance was in keeping with her social status outside. She was convicted of two crimes. Initially, she had been working as a bookkeeper in an office and was discovered as an embezzler. She went to County jail, being released after she completed her sentence. Shortly thereafter, her husband was discovered dead, floating in their swimming pool. It was alleged that she drowned him. That was the offense that put her in CIW.

Florence talked rapidly; she reminded me of a high strung woman I knew who never-stopped talking. What Florence said made sense but she was highly suspected by the staff members as being intellectually dangerous to the existing prison system. She was a rapid typist and had excellent secretarial skills. Philosophy books and other intellectual materials were her favorite reading materials. Social change was her main interest. She was talented at writing the right kind of letter, which was the way to get the ear of people in charge. Florence created numerous proposals or plans that were detailed and well thought out and were sent to Governor Brown or Director Enomoto. She had a connection with Enomoto because she was assistant secretary in the Superintendent's office when he was Acting Superintendent at CIW. We frequently had someone from the Department of Corrections investigating something based on a proposal or letter Florence had written.

In addition to working in the CIW library, Florence was assigned frequently to work in the front lobby of the Administration Building. Her work area was at a table next to the glass front door that was the door to freedom. She was a trustee and sold food tickets and other items to visitors. Mrs. West, Chair of Parole Board, was flustered by this because she thought Florence might see her auto license number and through connections could find her home address and harm her. The administrators and staff members at CIW had somewhat the same concern about certain residents seeing our license plate numbers. For this reason we did not like these women too close to the windows where our cars were parked. I could not find any solid reason to fear Florence. She liked to hang out around me and I thought she was a likable but complex person.

Florence was the spearhead of our initial college program. Actually, we would not have had the program if she had not done the work to get Chaffey College structured to conduct a mutual program with us. She was interested in work/study programs where residents could go out of the prison, live in a work/study environment and go to school. Florence ultimately obtained a scholarship to the University of California at Davis. Because Mrs. West was frightened of Florence, the Parole Board would not release her when there was no longer a reason for her to remain at CIW. For example, when Florence won her scholarship to UC Davis, to qualify for it she had to go there to register. Her Parole Hearing date was two weeks later, and the Parole Board would not give her two weeks' early release so she could register. She had to wait another semester to register. I concluded that Mrs. West knew Florence was an articulate person who could write a letter to the bureaucrats and be a potential threat. Florence thought most of the staff members were incompetent. We finally arranged for her parole and she did enroll at UC Davis.

PEARL: Over a weekend, I received telephone call saying that the Sheriff's Department had brought a woman named Pearl to CIW. She had been arrested at a motel for prostitution and robbery. She was being given a routine physical examination in the Reception Center when suddenly the doctor dropped his instruments. *My God, this is a man!* Here was Pearl, a woman with a penis! We learned that Pearl had started hormone treatments to become a female, when he was twelve years old, and never went through puberty. A Deputy Sheriff was summoned to return to CIW and Pearl quickly was hustled over to the California Institution for Men (CIM) where the Warden called the Corrections Department for confinement instructions.

Soon thereafter Pearl was moved from CIM to the California Medical Facility at Vacaville. This is the men's prison where gays and mentally-disturbed felons are imprisoned. The next week, Doctor Rowland, our psychiatrist, and I flew to Vacaville for a meeting with the physician who was the Warden of the prison. Pearl was brought into the room and that was the first chance I had to meet him (her?) I was prepared to see a gay man, but within a few minutes, I had no problem accepting Pearl as a female. This wasn't a man with female mannerisms at all but visibly a woman. She had a soft body, was curvaceous and pretty with no hair on her face. She was attractively manicured, was wearing a dress and displayed shapely legs. Her large, soulful eyes were swollen with tears. I talked with Pearl and her Counselor for about an hour. I could not imagine what the Corrections Department would do with this poor, unfortunate person, because essentially, this was a woman.

After some discussion I offered to take Pearl into CIW because initially at Vacaville the staff members had made her undress in front of an audience of inmates who were hooting at her body, staring at her breasts. Then Pearl was isolated in protective custody to shield her from being raped by the inmates. She wanted to be a seamstress, and CIW's sewing factory would be an excellent program placement for her. It seemed like an appropriate plan.

One other transsexual, Richard, was brought into the room. Richard looked like a man and acted like a gay man. He had gone through puberty before starting the sex change injections. He had large breasts, but he was almost six feet tall and well developed physically in the shoulders and arms. In looking at him, I was worried about our staff members being physically able to deal with someone that size. I decided we could not physically manage him at CIW, but offered to take

Pearl. Then intense discussion followed about what would be Pearl's programming, what if residents would try to rape Pearl, what if the media learned that a "person with a penis" was housed in the women's prison? How would I deal with that?

The outcome was that the Corrections Department decided to parole Pearl immediately because they became convinced there was no place in the system to accommodate her. What a weak solution! Richard remained at Vacaville.

IRMA: She was a resident I met outside my office the first day on the job. A plump woman in her sixties not quite five feet tall, she wore thick eyeglasses and was carrying a tape recorder (considered contraband in the prison.) She sidled up close to me and said in a squeaky voice *Hi, I'm Irma Kramer*. I thought maybe she was a teacher or a Counselor, because I wasn't yet aware that residents, other than those who worked in the Administration Building, had free access into that area. I said *Hello Irma Kramer. I'm Brook Carey*. She replied *So you're the new Superintendent? That's nice.* We chatted briefly and she went on her way.

About an hour later I was walking in the hall again and here was the same resident. She came up to me and said, *Hi, I'm Irma Kramer*, as if we hadn't met. Suddenly I realized that she was virtually blind and appeared to have mental problems. She should have been in the Psychiatric Treatment Unit (PTU.) The staff members did not know what to do with her, so they let her meander through the halls of the Administration Building. Wandering around was her therapy program. I contacted her Correctional Counselor. *If I find Irma Kramer and her tape recorder in the Ad Building again, I'm going to terminate someone.*

Her file was interesting to read. Irma and her husband had befriended an elderly couple who owned a motel, and by subversive means persuaded the couple to sign over to them the ownership of the motel. Then Irma murdered them with an axe and buried them in the basement of the motel under several feet of dirt and concrete. Her husband subsequently died; whether or not he was in prison I don't know. Because she was legally blind; her Counselor arranged a special college program and she was allowed to have the lectures on tape. She was studying Shakespeare. Since she could not read, it was probably the Plays that were on tape. She had not been assigned to PTU to receive the therapy she needed. I instructed her Counselor to assign her there and ultimately we arranged for her release into a halfway house where she was supervised. She had been at CIW almost twenty years.

STORMY: A trouble maker, Stormy was a Caucasian redhead about twenty-six. The staff members told me she was the most violent woman we had, and that intrigued me. I pulled her file and read it; she was convicted of credit card fraud.

I decided I would personally try to help her. Stormy was a very angry woman, always in some sort of a problem or getting a 115 for talking back or throwing something. She intimidated the staff members because she was tall and very intelligent. She was a suspected leader in the "Kill the Baby Killers" spray paint incident. She compounded her sentence through various infractions of the rules and the 115s kept growing in her file. It appeared that she never would be released in spite of her offense being relatively minor. (Only crimes against <u>persons</u> were considered to be major.)

The first time I met with her she was red-faced and hostile. *You are the PO-LEESE! I ain't talking to no PO-LEESE.* I hadn't thought of myself as being "police" so that took me aback. (Actually our Correctional Officers did have police powers.) In spite of her outbursts we continued to meet every week or two. I grew to like her and respect her positions. She was from Arizona and her parents kept in contact with her. She came from a middle-class, educated family and once her father phoned me and we talked about her. I was sympathetic toward him. When Stormy learned that I had talked with her father she threatened to get me fired. She angrily said *It is none of your business to discuss any of my business with my parents. How dare you? My file is confidential and you breached the confidentiality.* It had not occurred to me that it was not appropriate to talk to her father. I apologized and told her I was interested in helping her and so were her parents. *Perhaps I made a mistake in thinking you wanted to be helped,* I told her. That broke the ice and we continued the hourly sessions in my office.

Just before I left, I was able to persuade Stormy that she was on the staff's "bad list" and no matter what she did, no matter how innocuous the incident, the staff members might interpret her actions in a negative way and write her up. I told her *Your file is getting thicker by the month with 115s. Would you consider letting us transfer you to the Arizona women's prison where you are unknown? You could have a fresh start, and be closer to your family.* She finally agreed and we arranged a transfer shortly thereafter. On her transfer date she came into my office to say goodbye. She was happy to be moving closer to her parents and appreciated my help in arranging the transfer. Embarrassed, she shyly gave me a farewell note. *I'll never forget you,* it said. *Thank you so much Mrs. Carey for caring about me.* The note brought tears to my eyes. Each small success was particularly important to me.

NANCY: A large African American in her late twenties, Nancy was a former drug addict. She was confined in CIW for embezzlement. She was the secretary for the Residents' Council and also prepared the proposals for actions and activities that residents wanted. She was a mild person, and I liked her. Nancy was instrumental in keeping resident affairs moving along and helping to maintain relative calm on the campus. After parole, she planned to go to University of California at Davis on a prison exit program and then enroll at the University as a free person. She had no suitable clothing for her release. In our inventory of donated clothing, nothing fit her because of her size. I went to my sources in the community to find someone who would have the size clothing she needed and Nancy was pleased with the result. When it was time for her parole I called her into my office and told her I appreciated what she had done for CIW. *Thank you, Mrs. Carey. CIW has been a really good place for me. I'm glad I was here. I have learned a lot and will miss everybody.* I said *Good luck, Nancy. I hope I never see you again.* She continued to write to let me know she was getting along well and staying off drugs and out of trouble.

BARBARA: A Caucasian, Barbara was a licensed attorney, about forty. She dressed in expensive fashions; it was awhile before I learned that she wasn't an employee. She preferred riding jodhpurs, boots and suede jackets. She tried to help the Administration by confiding about activities in the resident population. I appreciated her attitude and felt favorable toward her. Just before she left on parole, she asked if I would be willing to testify in her behalf at the Los Angeles Bar Association Hearing that soon would be held to determine if her license to practice law should be reinstated. I agreed, and after receiving a letter of instruction from Barbara's attorney, I drove into Los Angeles for the Hearing.

The Hearing was held in a small courtroom where a panel of attorneys sat at the front of the room. I waited in an anteroom until my name was called. As I stood in the witness box, a clerk holding a Holy Bible administered the oath: *Do you swear to tell the truth, the whole truth and nothing but the truth, so help you God?* I said *Yes, I do.* After my identity was established for the record the first question was did I know that Barbara was a liar? I said I had no knowledge or experience about that. The next question was, assuming that Barbara was a liar, would I be willing to hire her as my attorney? I replied *Unconditionally, yes.* That answer surprised the attorney who was questioning me so he asked me to elaborate on my answer. I replied that because I had taken an oath of honesty on the Holy Bible, I assumed that the Hearing was being conducted under Christian rules of "God" and my understanding of those rules was that when a wrongdoer confesses her "sin" and then completes her punishment she is forgiven. Therefore, I could find no reason not to hire Barbara as my attorney.

The panel members were astonished. After conferring for a few minutes, they decided to reinstate Barbara's license to practice law. Her attorney followed me out of the room. *Mrs. Carey, where did you get that fantastic argument? It just was logical*, I replied. Barbara was very appreciative of my creative testimony. She asked me if together we could write a book about CIW. I briefly considered that idea, but when Barbara made an unexpected pass at me I said *No thank you*. After being paroled, rather than return to practicing law Barbara purchased a motel in Palm Springs and promoted it as a luxury resort for lesbians.

CAROL and GABBY: Carol was African American woman with bright yellow hair. She worked in the Cosmetology program where she once attacked another resident with a razor and almost killed her. She was a habitual criminal with an ugly disposition. Carol was having a lesbian relationship with another resident, Gabby, a Caucasian, who was mannish. Those two openly made a display of their relationship. Gabby also was dangerous; she had little self control. Those types are the residents to worry about, because they would just as soon kill you as look at you. I became interested in Gabby and worked with her because the staff considered her to be an "impossible" resident. The Counseling staff had almost given up on her rehabilitation. It seemed that she always was in trouble. When she finally was paroled she realized she would have to leave Carol behind. This had not occurred to her that Carol was remaining while she was being released. We had several conversations with her because she did not want to leave. Finally I told her *Go back to your family and get a job. Then you can earn some money and can help Carol when she is paroled. Just get yourself established.* I felt exasperated with Gabby but concealed my feelings.

Gabby wanted to return to visit Carol but ex-felons are not allowed to visit a prison, or write to people in prison while they are on parole. That turned out to be a difficult situation because those two were love partners, just like a married couple. When Gabby was released, she phoned two or more times a day to ask about Carol and to try to get messages to her. Finally, in desperation, she committed a crime so she could come back into the prison. She returned to CIW and she and Carol lived happily in the system. Much of the recidivism (returning to prison) at CIW was because a lesbian is released who then wants to return to her partner, so she commits a crime. Since CIW was the only women's prison in the State, it was a safe bet that she would be remanded there.

ETHEL: She was one of my most interesting residents. She was a "little old lady school teacher" type, a duck out of water in CIW. She was Caucasian, about fifty, quiet, liked to sit in her room crocheting and listening to classical music. Ethel could not accept being in prison and could not relate to any of it. She was frightened of the other residents. Her crime was a strange act indeed. She had injected cherry candies with poison and sent a box of them to the Los Angeles District Attorney. When I learned what her offense was, I thought the staff members were kidding me. Her records didn't reveal a motive and my impression of Ethel was that she seemed completely harmless. She was content just to do her time and she never worried about or anticipated a parole date.

LUCY: An African American, Lucy was a lesbian, about thirty, with smooth skin and very pretty. She was languid, graceful and dressed in the latest fashions. Lucy had escaped a couple of years before by climbing over the perimeter fence. She walked down the road into the nearby town of Chino where she hailed a cab. When the cab driver did not follow her instructions, she pulled out a knife and stabbed him in the neck. Soon she was back to prison on that offense, and the instigator behind many of the problems we had. She was clever and seldom was caught making mischief. She knew how to make other residents take the rap for her actions. I disliked Lucy and avoided contacts with her.

Once when Lucy was in the PTU lockup she put an illegal drug kit into her vagina to hide it. Two weeks later we discovered it because of the odor. I went to the lockup to confront her. I said *Lucy, I've been interested in helping you, but think what you're doing to yourself. I won't go to bat for you and help you get ready for parole if you do things like that.* She acted sweet and charming as though nothing had happened. I figured that Lucy had never had good role models in her life, so I arranged for a "friend" to come in. There was an outside volunteer group called M-2 that matched residents in prison with people from the outside. I asked M-2 to send a "friend" to talk with her and try to influence her. Because our Counseling services did not have the staff to provide individual counseling, the M-2 program seemed like a good course of action in this case. The "friend" was helpful in getting Lucy to think about and plan for her future but that didn't prevent her from being a trouble maker during the December disturbance.

I could not give up on any resident, even when the staff members had written her off. I could not imagine coming to work and just keeping residents in a holding pattern, not thinking about ways to help them. I came from a career where I counseled and helped people. I changed their lives, and it never occurred to me that I could not do that with prison residents. I was responsible for their custody, but essentially I am a humanistic, counselor type person. What I only learned later was that in California only ten percent of the people who commit crimes ever are caught and prosecuted, and of those, only about ten percent ever go to prison. Prisons, essentially then, contain the worst offenders—people who deserve to be there. It was hard to accept this. I regarded almost every resident as a worthy individual. I was interested in all of those I encountered.

I believed about eighty percent of the residents should be in prison to protect society from them. The other twenty percent were women who each had committed only a single crime of passion. One of our residents killed the man she lived with who had beaten her for twenty years which is an example of a crime that does not make the perpetrator dangerous to society. People have asked me what the inmates are really like as if committing a crime makes people greatly different. Many of the residents I learned to know seemed just like people on the outside, friendly, capable and many of them harmless. It was not that difficult to relate with most of them.

Male/Female Relationships

After one resident left CIW and went into the County jail to be on trial for a previous offense, she told the authorities that a CIW male staff member had molested her. This was described as a male staff member who tried to put his hand on her breast. I immediately summoned the investigating unit from the Corrections Department. There were units of these investigators stationed around the State to assist the prison Administrators. Our investigator was Fred Sawyer. My instructions were to contact Fred if I had any reason to think there was a problem with staff members. The investigators respected me because they knew I am a straight arrow who did not try a cover-up of any alleged malpractice. When other Wardens were suspected of trying to cover up suspicious events they would sometimes say *This situation doesn't need investigating.* I bent over backward for the investigators which made them feel important. I knew that some residents were making overtures to the male staff members but to my knowledge the men were not making sexual overtures to the residents. Fortunately, Fred completed a detailed investigation and failed to find any truth to that resident's accusation.

I never had complaints of this nature except that one incident. In prison, it is common for inmates to try to strike back at the system by alleging a staff member was making an indecent approach, or worse. Our male staff members were aware of that so they made sure they were not alone with the residents and avoided any kind of a situation that was questionable. Usually there were other staff members around, so a man would have to be careless to be alone with a resident. For example, all the Correctional Counselors' office walls were glass, so there wasn't any visual privacy in them, and the offices were at the end of the day rooms where there was constant coming and going.

Residents were bold about making approaches to visitors. On one occasion, I was taking a good looking young male visitor on a campus tour. While we were touring, a couple of residents were skulking along behind the trees saying *"Pssst, want to go with me into the bushes?"* while making obscene gestures to him. He was astonished! I did not know whether they were kidding or serious, but such behavior certainly was unnerving to visiting men.

Sexual contact between residents was less difficult to achieve. Each resident had a single room and was locked in at night. During the day they were out of their rooms walking around to various programs, classes and the dining rooms. In my first days on the job, I enjoyed the panorama view from my office's picture window—the campus with the swimming pool at the far end, the cottages and residents lounging around on the grass. Looking closely, I noticed that a few were lying on top of a partner, fondling each other, hand holding and stroking each other's bodies. That was commonplace when I arrived. On one occasion, Bill was visiting me in my office. We both noticed from the picture window, some "hot and heavy" activity between two residents on a nearby bench. I lamented there was little to be done. By the time staff members were summoned to break it up, the incident would be over. Bill briefly thought about this and then suggested *Call the grounds keeper and have him turn on the sprinklers!* That "cooled off" the incident. I began using this remedy as my secret weapon with much success.

The staff members were accustomed to overlooking such behavior so they scarcely reacted to it. Apparently I was the only one who responded to it. I would say *Look at that*, and they would say *Look at what?* Thinking back, there was not a lot of overt lesbian activity because there were enough staff members and residents who disapproved, and there were enough "snitches" to keep us informed of such activity. Lesbian activity in California is illegal only in a prison. One day a group of women with megaphones appeared outside the perimeter fence. They proceeded to march around the front of the Administration Building shouting *GAY IS COOL! GAY IS COOL!* I asked Ron Burke to find out who they were and what they wanted. I was ready to meet with them and consider their demands. It turned out that they had no demands, and did not want to meet with me. Apparently, they just wanted to march around yelling. Frankly, I do not disapprove of homosexual behavior outside of prison. I am not a judgmental person. So much for that!

Many of the residents were rather unattractive women however we had a number of appealing female staff members. We did have situations where a Correctional Officer would get involved with a staff member of the opposite sex. Outsiders think that female prison inmates are an attraction for certain males. But most staff members were regarded as adversaries by residents. To them, Correctional Officers are the police, so it was difficult to build any trust with the residents. The only incident that came to my attention was that false allegation made by a former resident on trial by the County. No residents contended that men were spying on them when they were in the shower or scantily clad. They surely would have told me as they wrote me letters all the time.

About seventy percent of the staff members were female and well-suited for their positions. Most of the male Correctional Officers were police-type people who really liked the idea of being macho opposite tough guys in the men's prisons. Then, sadly for them, they are transferred to the women's prison. I knew of no male Correctional Officers who really wanted to work at CIW. They felt it was like a demotion or punishment. A number of the men transferred to CIW had so much seniority that they had accrued many hours of compensatory and vacation time in addition to sick leave. Therefore they seldom were on the active duty rolls. That is why CIW was continuously understaffed. Most of the male Correctional Officers at CIW had been transferred from prisons in northern California. When they had to move to Southern California for personal reasons often CIM at Chino would not take them so CIW was their only alternative for continued employment with the Department of Corrections. Male staff members were carefully screened before being hired. There were no male staff members who displayed lack of self control. We gave special attention to the selection of male Correctional Officers who were assigned to custody in the cottages.

June Wardens' Meeting

My second Wardens' meeting was held in Las Vegas, Nevada in early June. The Corrections Department arranged for security guards to assure the Wardens' safety in such a public place. After the first day of meetings, we were free to enjoy the gaming at the hotel. Las Vegas offered a relaxed atmosphere for the Wardens to socialize. Tom Stone, Warden of San Quentin, was a big bear of a fellow. He was helpful in discussing some of my concerns and trying to help me find fixes for them. The tours I had of men's prisons when I first arrived were interesting, but actually there is little in common regarding operations between men's and women's prisons.

I am not a gambler but slot machines always fascinate me. I had some modest winnings and had enjoyed the noise and action in the hotel's casino. Later in the evening I was headed toward my room when I spotted Jake Gunn, Warden of Folsom, at the bar. I slid onto the stool next to him and checked him out. Jake was clearly stressed and soon the reason became apparent. He said that Folsom was housing Charles Manson and that some of the Manson "Family" members, led by Lynette "Squeaky" Fromme, were appearing outside the walls of the prison on a regular basis. They were demonstrating for Manson's release. Charles Manson is a convicted serial killer who has become an icon of evil. In the late 1960s, Manson founded a hippie cult group known as the Manson "Family" whom he manipulated in brutally killing others on his behalf.

Jake confided that he feared for the safety of his family. I suggested that he consider transferring Charlie to Soledad or San Quentin to foil any escape plans for him that might be planned by the "Family." I was the newcomer, so what could I possibly know? But Jake was energized by that suggestion and immediately felt calmer. Two days later I read in the newspaper that Charlie had been transferred to San Quentin. I never heard from Jake about that.

Manson Family Threat

In early July, the Federal Bureau of Investigation (FBI) in Los Angeles received an undated letter postmarked at Chicago containing threats against unidentified persons if certain specified members of the Charles Manson "Family" were not released from prison by July 12. The female members of the "Family" referred to in the letter were residents at CIW. The letter quickly was forwarded to the Department of Corrections and then to the respective Wardens.

Here is that letter verbatim—spelling and punctuation errors intact.

Dear Piggies [sic]

We are giving you your first, last and only chance to save yourselves and your whole fuckin [sic] town of PIGS and crucifiers from a massacre a thousand times the tate.[sic] Our LOVE has been violated and caged only because he tried to show you bastards how to get over.

Our LOVE is not going to suffer for you anymore. What we did was set those PIGS free they were grateful to die it was beautiful for both them and us it was done with real love for them, and because you PIGS do not know what love or living really is all about you and all the other PIGS sent our LOVE and our sisters to your cage Love has always meant to be free and our LOVE has to and will be free if we have to kill every PIG in and around L.A. for miles around until theres [sic] no one left.

This is a demand for the release of Charles Manson, Charles Watson, Susan Atkins, Leslie Van Houten, Patricia Krenwinkle, Mary Brunner, Robert Beausoleil, Steve Grogan, Bruce Davis. And it is the only one your going to get if you do not release our LOVE and our other brothers and sisters the shit is going to come man and come down hard we swear if you do not release them that all of you PIGS are going to need canoes to paddle through the blood that is going to fill your streets.

Sure we did the Tate thing and the others but they had to be done they had to realize, get it going and yet it was only the PIGS who thought we were wrong but we weren't we did not hurt those PIGS we helped them, helped them become free of themselves because they themselves were hurting theirselves.

[*sic*]. We did them the biggest favor anyone ever did them, and instead of being grateful all you PIGS did was to put our LOVE in a cage our LOVE our GOD the one and only one who truly understands and cares for everybody.

Well baby the karmas turning and the time is now your time is we are giving you exactly four weeks from today to release our family or we're all coming back and were coming down hard. If you have any ideas that this is some kind of joke keep your eyes on the callender [*sic*] if by July 12th our LOVE and our family is not released then on July 13th you'll find your first five dead PIGGIES and five more every day until all are realeased [*sic*] we already know who the first five will be. If you choose to ignore this be our guest.[*sic*] we'll just keep decreasing the amount of PIGS until you listen [*sic*] just ask the Bug he know us real well [*sic*] he'll tell you whether we'll do it or not. A family needs to be together and it needs its [*sic*] father [*sic*] you have taken ours from us and until we get ours back we'll be taking many fathers away from their families forever.

Some of us are there now preparing in case you do not cooperate which we do not think you will at first this is why we have already designated exactly who the first five will the they are some of your celebrity type of PIGS the singer who can't sing any more for one after all when we do the first five we want to be sure that they are the type of PIGGIES that your [*sic*] very familiar with. For the last time release our LOVE and our family by the 12th of July or get your first five dead PIGS by the 13th.

REMEMBER HE WENT TO YOUR CAGE FOR US AND WE'LL GIVE OUR LIVES TO GET HIM OUT IF NECESSARY.

All our love [*sic*]

The Family

I received a copy of this letter from the FBI around the third of July, and it was stamped "THE CONTENTS OF THIS COMMUNICATION ARE RESTRICTED AND CONFIDENTIAL." I read it several times then placed it in my handbag. I felt frightened thinking what could happen. I needed to consult Bill about this. It never occurred to me to call Walt Cooper, my boss. That's because I only spoke to him a few times during the months since I came aboard. He was virtually a non-existent resource to me.

When I arrived home that Friday evening, Bill met me at the door and seemed to tell at a glance that something was not all right. As I was enjoying my much anticipated embrace with him he stood back and said *Sweetheart, is something going wrong at the "joint"?* I could have kept the entire matter from him but he was my advisor and protector so I handed him the Manson letter. After he finished reading it for the second time, I told him my concerns for all the Corrections Department personnel and particularly for our personal safety at home. We felt reasonably confident for the safety of our children as they were residing at various schools. He put down the letter, leaned back and got that far-away look in his eyes. I knew at that moment he was developing a security plan for us. Bill's protective nature was very comforting to me and I did not hesitate to turn over to him the planning of the next actions.

During the rest of the evening, Bill asked many questions about my movements around CIW, going to work, securing my car, leaving the facility, driving home and our family activities while at home. This was an opportunity for him to raise the issue more emphatically concerning my choice of where we were living and our telephone number and address being listed in the Riverside telephone directory. While helping me clear the dinner table he commented *Living virtually in the middle of nowhere and telling the whole world where we live are two of the weakest links in any security plan. For your protection, we're going to enlist some outside help right away, specifically from the County Sheriff and the Riverside PD.*

I thought to myself, what a lucky day it was for me to marry not only my soul mate but also a Green Beret who was trained in defensive and offensive intelligence activities. He always made me feel happy and secure. Before bedtime, we discussed what he referred to as the "drop dead" date of Monday, July 13, specified in the Manson letter. Bill had given the situation careful thought before he said *If you can assume that date, which is speculative, there is about a week plus to beef up our domestic security and for you to develop alternative routes to and from work. Also, you should watch for anything out of pattern or out of place at the "joint" particularly concerning the Manson girls.*

The following Monday morning while finding a different route to work, I actually felt empowered to know we were not going to sit around wringing our hands while waiting for the grim reapers. After arriving at CIW and going through the morning briefings and meetings, I withdrew to my office to develop a finely tuned security plan that would not alarm the staff. This was difficult as I believed only the Wardens and the "top brass" knew about this threat. In later retrospect, it was reasonable to assume that my two "loyal" Deputies probably knew about it through their back channel communications with Walt Cooper. It was an unfortunate situation where I could not tell them and they would not tell me. It would have been helpful to have their expertise in this situation. I did initiate a call to several of the other Wardens emphasizing we should be in direct contact should a Manson-related threat materialize at any of the prisons.

That afternoon I put on a brave face and called a meeting of my key staff. I told them that after four months on the job I was ready to take a detailed look at the security practices at CIW. This meeting was not to discuss training program content, type of foods served, rehab projects or grounds maintenance. This meeting was all about security of our residents and what were CIW's strengths and weaknesses. I made a point that the family visitations and social events appeared to present many gaps in our expected level of security. Also, a closer look should be taken at the Special Case residents that Governor Brown had instructed me to watch personally.

I asked the staff at this meeting to go to their departments and take a close look at the existing security measures and what could be done to improve them. They were to report back to the conference room in twenty four hours with their findings and recommendations. Prior to adjournment, I gave them some parting advice: *Don't look only at what the residents are doing, consider what they're not doing.* In effect, I was telling them to look at the pattern of activities to determine is there any departure from business as usual. Was there something about a particular resident that seemed to be out of step? I began to feel confident that I was on the right track.

That evening after negotiating another alternate route home, I told Bill what I had accomplished at CIW and that I believed my actions would increase security without the staff members' knowledge of the Manson letter. Bill told me he had been busy also with plans to augment our home security. He had made arrangements, in my name, for a meeting with the Riverside County Sheriff and a Riverside Police Department representative. As he did not have my schedule, he left it up to Beverly, my secretary, to call the phone numbers he provided and set up the meetings. He suggested if he could be included in these meetings, it would be helpful.

Prior to our dinner time that evening Bill told me there was a new routine regarding the parking of my company car at home. Fortunately the house had iron gates at the head of the driveway that separated the garage from the street. He had cleared the second bay of our garage to accommodate the company car. We went outside and, in a ceremonial fashion, moved the car through the gates and into the garage. With the garage door and the gate locked we resumed our happy hour on the patio. It wasn't until later I found out he was concerned about a bomb being planted underneath my car. The following day I confirmed the two meetings that Bill had instigated with the law enforcement agencies.

That afternoon my key staff members reassembled in the conference room and I did my best to keep them focused on the reason for this second meeting.

Specifically, what were their recommendations to enhance the security of the residents? The first recommendation that came to the table was that the physical accountability of residents during a typical day should be increased. Without name tags or prison garb, the staff members had the virtually impossible task of knowing every resident by sight. I detected increased spirit of cooperation between the Correctional staff members and the Counselors. The second recommendation was that staff members were unanimous in agreement that family visitations and social events required much closer scrutiny and more thorough searches of visitors. They really went to work on this issue but unfortunately their new diligence came around to bite us at the upcoming Christmas season. I was pleased though to observe the developing cooperation among the staff members.

The next day, Bill and I met with the Riverside County Sheriff. While waiting in his outer office, we admired the silver-festooned riding saddle used by the Sheriff in ceremonial rides and parades with his posse. Apparently this was customary in California, especially at the annual Rose Parade. After sitting down with the Sheriff, I brought up the fact that there were increasing threats on my staff members, particularly focused on the Manson girls in my custody. These concerns had to be expressed without revealing the existence of the Manson letter. We told the Sheriff of our isolated home site and asked what, if anything, his department could do to enhance our safety from the members of the Manson clan still on the loose and hiding out in caves in Inyo County, a hundred miles or so north of Riverside.

The Sheriff was attentive and understanding and allowed he had jurisdiction in our area but suggested that our first line of defense should be the Riverside Police Department. Armed with that information, we went to the next appointment at the police department.

After arriving, we met with a detective and recounted the same concerns as we had detailed to the Sheriff. The detective agreed, based on what we told him, that our isolated house location did present a greater risk for home intrusions. At this point Bill expressed another concern. He was an expert pistol shot, having competed in various national competitions. Therefore any break in, particularly at night, would have to be considered a deadly threat on our lives with the consequences of shoot first and ask questions later. What if this intruder would turn out to be just a kid looking to steal a television set? The detective said he would discuss this scenario with his superiors and get back with us with an answer. Before we left we did get a promise of increased police patrols on our street and unscheduled police helicopter flyovers at night. In addition if we believed we were in danger we only had to call a certain telephone number at the police department and say the words: *Tava Lane*. This signaled a code-three police dispatch to our home address on Tava Lane in Riverside.

While driving back to the house, Bill looked at me and said *I think we had a successful day in getting the additional police protection for the house. Now it's up to me to fine-tune the plan for our own personal security.* That evening at home I started to see Bill's security plan unfold. Cocktail time was moved inside as soon as it was dark to the degree that our rear fence was not clearly visible. While sitting on the patio it was then I noticed the hand gun tucked in his belt.

It was check and double check all the door and window locks. Fortunately we had decorative wrought iron bars over most of the windows. Another part of the plan was to make sure the front and back porch lights, driveway gate lights and garage door lights were turned on. As the house was built in the shape of a square U our bedroom was on the opposite side of the patio from the living room. By leaving a light on in the living/dining area we had an unobstructed view of that part of the house across the patio from our bedroom.

The rest of the week was spent practicing defensive driving techniques that Bill taught me going back and forth from the prison and getting more involved in the daily activities of my staff members and the residents. My phone conversations with the other Wardens revealed nothing of special note or alarm. As we approached the weekend I wondered what the following Monday the 13th would bring.

Meanwhile Bill had been enhancing our home security with the installation of exterior flood lights at key locations around the house. All these lights could be turned on by just two switches, one in the kitchen and one in our bedroom. While sitting on our patio on Friday night before darkness mandated our retreat into the house, we discussed the impending do or die date of the following Monday. I was tempted that we should get out of town over the weekend but, as the threat date was the following Monday, that would serve no purpose other than to take me out of the loop during a critical time. We talked about this and Bill said *Look, we've done all that's feasible short of hiring armed guards and living in a fortress. We can't be hostages to this situation. Let's go on a date Saturday night and have a good time while keeping our eyes and ears open.*

We did go out to one of our favorite hideaway restaurants. We both needed an intimate place to look at one another, hold hands and remember our romantic meeting in a similar restaurant a few years ago in a place far away. When we arrived home, I was witness to another of Bill's security measures. I was told to stay in the car with the windows rolled up and the engine running while he circled the house with his flashlight, checking his fish line segments he had glued to the doors and their frames to determine if any had been broken indicating a probable intruder. With the "all clear" we entered the house and headed for our nesting place.

The following Monday, July 13, came and went without incident. Bill had even driven me to work in our own car. I was nervous and anxious all day, waiting for some bad news by phone, but nothing happened. As the days and weeks went by without any hostile actions against Department of Corrections' personnel, it was easy to fall into complacency. Bill and I discussed this at length with the conclusion that we would not be held hostages to a veiled threat and life should go on, while keeping our personal security measures in place.

When sitting on our patio a few weeks after the threat date, Bill, with gun in his belt suddenly said *I've had years in the military of looking over my shoulder with a gun in my hand. Here it is 1975 in sunny California and it seems like I'm in a war zone while having to protect my soul mate. Do we really need to be doing this?* My first instinct was to agree because I love Bill deeply and want to please him. But I voluntarily accepted this tough position and I expected to honor my contract. Relenting, Bill told me that I had his continuing support in whatever situation this takes us. I did have guilty feelings. I was selfishly gratifying myself in my position as Superintendent and thereby imposing on Bill whose new mission was to keep me safe. I felt conflicted, thinking that perhaps I was being disloyal to Bill, but torn because of my loyalty to CIW and the need to keep my word.

Challenges to be Managed

Heading Off a Disturbance. I had arrived in March, and by June I was telling the Deputy Superintendents *I believe we are going to have a disturbance at CIW. This really is an unsettled situation.* It had been that way long before I came. I did not put it down in writing or make a commotion, I just kept saying it. I believe Jerry Enomoto may have suspected that there was going to be a disturbance at CIW. So the Corrections Department decided to find an "outside woman" to take the fall when the riot came down. Each time I talked to superiors I would say *We need adequate staff, better facilities.* When I look back on it I think why didn't I know within thirty days that the job situation was almost unworkable? There were so many small details that had to be addressed as a top priority each day that it was almost impossible to address to the real issues effectively and in a timely way.

In 1975, CIW was considered by outsiders to be one of the model prisons in the country. Its size—seven hundred fifty female felons—made it different from others. In the Nevada women's prison there were about forty inmates; Arizona might have had up to sixty. They could not have broad offerings of programs. Their thinking was with forty female residents, let's teach a crocheting class. The problems arise for these small female felon populations because they have every type of woman, every level of custody, every type of crime, all combined into one place, and because of the small size, administrators cannot offer broad programs for rehabilitation.

Parenting in Prison. I was requested by the Corrections Department to institute a program so that CIW could accommodate residents' babies and toddlers being housed here. There was a new California law that a woman may have her child less than two years of age in prison with her. It doesn't say she can, it says she may. That was the big movement just starting in 1975. At the time I resigned, I was being sued by a resident who wanted to have her baby with her. She was depending on that statute. Imagine babies in this under-staffed, poorly maintained facility. The thinking behind this is if a child is born in the prison, or the woman is sentenced while she's pregnant and says she wants to breast-feed her baby, that baby may be breast-fed until approximately age two so the mother and child should not be separated. I support mothers and babies being together but CIW in those days had many tough and dangerous residents, and no practical way to isolate them from anyone. I assigned to Shirley, my former secretary now in charge of Special Projects, to do initial planning of the proposed new program.

About eighty percent of women in prison have children under age eighteen. Arranging for caregivers for the children is a difficult situation. Many women believe being "mother" is a full time job and therefore being incarcerated denies their basic mothering instinct. Some of those women withdraw from their children, believing that if the situation isn't "perfect" it is unacceptable. Caretaking by family members is usually more out of obligation than wanting to take responsibility for the children. Although many of the mothers demonstrated fitness as a parent, due to circumstances beyond their control, their children were placed in the welfare system. Eventually mothers could lose any relationship with their children. Often, well-meaning caretakers would distance the children from their mothers in an effort to maintain continuity for the children. This would play out especially hard during rare visiting days when the caretaker would bring the children for a brief visit.

Last March, as Bill was finishing his chores packing for the move to California, he sent our cat, Shadow on a plane to be with me. I brought Shadow to my office because I did not want to leave him in the Pine Tree Motel to wander away. Staff members warned me that we had a resident who killed animals. She would capture stray cats or birds and break their necks or throw them against the plate glass windows. I was concerned she would capture my cat and stomp it to death so Shadow then went to a boarding facility until Bill arrived. With small animals at potential risk one can imagine my thoughts about security in having small children living at CIW. It became a moot point as there was no money in the budget at that time to set up such a program. Fortunately, programs like this are common in women's prisons today.

Staff Training Seminars. In July, Roland Wood, Superintendent of the California Rehabilitation Center, the co-ed substance abuse treatment prison, invited me to participate in a training seminar for his prison's supervisory staff. I enjoyed getting back into the traces of training/teaching and the opportunity to expand beyond my daily routine at CIW. The thank you letter he sent to me renewed my confidence.

"I have heard numerous comments about your presentation and they were all very good. In fact, I sat in for your final session and I enjoyed it very much myself. I felt that the content of your presentation contained very pertinent information that our

supervisors should be able to utilize. They seemed to think this also. Incidentally, Lujan, my training officer informed me that you were singled out as the most dynamic and knowledgeable speaker of all our guest speakers, so congratulations for a job well done."

Roland Wood sent a copy of this letter to Director Enomoto and I had hopes that other opportunities to conduct training in the Corrections Department system would follow. I was disappointed that nothing came of it.

Based upon that feedback from Roland, I planned and presented several training seminars for CIW staff that were well received. I held several classes for residents with upcoming parole dates focusing on job-hunting and interviewing techniques. I also did some one-on-one informal career counseling for a few residents who were preparing for release. I really enjoyed getting back into that role however briefly. But I knew that other responsibilities took precedence.

Squeaky Fromme. On Wednesday, September 3, two agents from President Gerald Ford's Secret Service paid a visit to CIW. They wanted to know if we had any information about any person threatening the life of the President. They did not mention that President Ford was planning a visit to Sacramento on September 5. If I had known that, I would have told them that some women of the Manson "Family" were living in Sacramento and were threatening to kill prison officials. When they donned red robes and appeared outside various prisons, we all knew that killing was on their agenda. Lynette "Squeaky" Fromme was the leader of the Sacramento group. I wasn't very helpful in answering their questions because I was focused upon CIW residents who might be a threat rather than on outsiders.

On the morning of Friday, September 5, Squeaky Fromme went to Sacramento's Capital Park dressed in a long red robe and armed with a .45 Colt semi-automatic that she pointed at President Ford. She was restrained by Secret Service agents and arrested. At CIW, we heard an early radio broadcast "scoop" reporting that a woman in a long red robe had stepped forward from the crowd and pointed a gun at President Ford. We knew who that woman was before the agents did. Following her lengthy trial in which she received a life sentence for the attempted assassination of the President, Squeaky was remanded to the Federal prison system. We were relieved that the Federal crime took precedence so she was unlikely to be imprisoned at CIW. It is reported that although she has been eligible for parole since 1985 she consistently has waived her right to a hearing.

Senate Confirmation. Months after the fact, in early September, on the way to the Senate Confirmation Hearing in Sacramento I thought about my March meeting with Governor Brown. *Your job consists of three challenges: Keep those felons in there; keep them healthy; if there is time, do what you can about rehabilitation.* Those words were always in the front of my mind, so when I arrived for the Confirmation Hearing, I focused primarily on custody and health; rehabilitation was an elusive objective. The unsaid philosophy of the system was: prisons cannot rehabilitate felons, they must rehabilitate themselves.

It was early evening and I was alone. As this was just an overnight trip Bill and I decided that he should remain in Riverside and hold the fort. I walked through Capitol Park, the same park where Squeaky Fromme had accosted President Ford. As I ascended the steps of the Capital Building for my 7:30 P.M. Confirmation Hearing I so wished Bill could have been there for that special support. It was then I observed Harold Williams standing near the door. *I thought you might like some company,* he offered. I was pleased to see him. He toured me through the Capitol Building, ending in a small ante room. I had seen that room on the late TV news the previous night; it was the room in which Senate Hearings are held. Seated on a platform were four people. I had researched who the panel members would be, who they represented and what axes they might have to grind, so I was alert. I had been Superintendent for six months and engrossed with the job. The Confirmation Hearing was so far after the fact that it wasn't especially significant to me except I thought what will I do if I am not confirmed? There was little point in being nervous about that. I would deal with whatever came next.

When my name was called, I stepped forward and was ushered to a chair in front of the panel members. To my surprise no significant questions were asked. I expected to hear what is your opinion about …? How many years' experience do you have in managing a large organization? How are things going down there? What are the problems at CIW? Amazing! Within a few minutes I was confirmed unanimously. The entire Hearing seemed to be a farce. It really accomplished very little. But I was relieved that it was finished. One more hurdle behind me! What would the next major challenge be?

Meeting Charles Manson

I looked forward to the quarterly Wardens' Meetings because my fellow Wardens were helpful and friendly. I think the Wardens considered me a novelty and not a threat to their masculinity. I could try out ideas on them and get honest feedback. Early September brought the Wardens together for a meeting at San Quentin prison. Several of us were given a tour of the prison and the legendary Gas Chamber. That was interesting from a clinical point of view. The metal seat like chair where the condemned man is strapped was specifically designed to circulate the gas from underneath the device for quick inhalation. The lighting was dim. I wondered if female inmates were put to death there, since CIW had no such capacity. I hoped never to learn the answer to that.

The second day, we were having lunch in the Staff Cafeteria. Seated next to a friendly man in street clothes, I asked him what his job at San Quentin was. He replied *I'm Charlie Manson's Counselor. Would you like to meet him?* With little thought I said I would. Curiosity was driving me. I felt no fear at the prospect of facing Manson. I decided I would try to convince Charlie to stop contacting the "girls" because they just wanted to do their time quietly and work toward earning paroles. The Counselor escorted me to the special wing at San Quentin where the notorious and dangerous prisoners are held. When we appeared in the anteroom, the Correctional Officer on duty was visibly astonished. Apparently I was the first female ever to visit that special wing. The Counselor introduced me as Superintendent of CIW and the Officer immediately relaxed and smiled saying *Are you here to see Charlie?*

The special wing consisted of two rows of barred cells, back to back, with a hallway on each side in front of the cells. Windows lined the outside walls of the wing on both sides so residents could look through the bars across the hallway to see outside. Between the backs of the two rows of cells was a narrow "alley" so staff members could repair the toilets that residents sometimes plugged with refuse. The cells' back walls had steel doors in the center of each cell with 10"x12" barred windows in the doors. There were about sixteen cells on each side and Manson's cell was in the center of these. The Counselor and the Officer decided it was unsafe for me to walk in the hallway in front of the cells that had floor to ceiling bars but rather I should visit with Charlie through the tiny window in the rear steel door in the "alley." As I followed the Counselor through the narrow "alley" behind the cells, inmates peering out of the tiny windows in their doors began to call out to me *Hey, Lady, come back and talk to me. Hey, Lady!*

The Counselor stopped abruptly in front of one of the steel doors. Looking through the little barred window he said, *Charlie, get up and put your pants on. There's a lady here to see you.* In a minute, he stepped back, motioned me to look in the window and introduced me to Charlie. There he was a slight unshaven man, bare-chested, wearing jeans and a knitted cap. He looked to be about 5' 5" tall, and about 120 lbs. The cell smelled like a bear cage at the zoo because Charlie had smeared his feces on the walls. The entire scene was difficult to manage.

Gathering my composure, I told Charlie that I was in charge of the "girls" who were imprisoned at CIW and that their message to him was to stop writing to them and let them do their time in peace. Charlie rolled his eyes and said *Well how is Sadie Mae Glutz* (Susan Atkins) *doin'? She's a real sweetheart. And what about Katie* (Patricia Krenwinkle) *my quiet one?* He didn't ask about Leslie Van Houten. I replied *All the girls are doing well, but please stop trying to contact them. They just want to forget about you.*

Then Charlie began to ramble. His words and sentences did not make sense. He said *You people took my blood and put it in the sky and when it flowed down on the judge, then you know about my pain.* Charlie spoke like this, meaninglessly, for almost an hour. His ranting made no sense. I can't remember exactly all that Charlie said so I have inserted some of Charlie's later writing just to give you a flavor of his disjointed thoughts and words.

> *Secret, and the SS secrets and sacred, is a synonymous viewpoint when you look at it from the dead. Everything that was never told and held to the death, and was killed, martyred hearts to hold and held forth to the death that becomes a viewpoint, secret holy ghost.*
>
> *We the mind think, and are thought-there we are men of truth, righteous brothers' honor and had no way of knowing things and the ways kept from us. We all looked to death row where we thought brothers were being kept. We looked up to the strongest images, to the father. Gods [sic] mind in the flesh. Old cowboys, heroes, past wars and even bandits, crooks and revolutionists.*
>
> *We look for the patriarch soldier as we were told and shown on TV [sic] and movies. They died for our rights and all we thought was 'love and real'. Then the end of acts and stars changed our minds. We saw the covers were not real. The cover is real but like rubber apples—they look good but you can't eat them.*
>
> *What was kept secret or concealed as we lived our lives in 2 world wars, cover ups-past.*

> On from the money heads, all the good real and love was murdered right before our eyes. We saw it but we were told and taught and we had no way to find out but to go through it. Our Souls the soul kept calling the eyes of the soul—seen one thing, our souls were going one way and your words and ways were going the other—so we ended up on death row in a war that started before our granddads were born.
>
> The egg broke in 1969. The courtroom I was in, in the 1940's when the USA was calling war a crime and crime became a war my court room became. When the Manson cult went to death row to redeem the brother, we thought was there it was there but in the graves. The secrets and keeping word true Manson was raised up in prison not knowing that the people that kept their word were hung and put to death and that there was only a movie left, and money slaves. I hold the worlds in English and the secrets of the bottom line underworld. SS, death head cult, death, will of revolution and pirate USN George Washington, USA, USSR, China, Japan and Germany and all the good Indians.
>
> Life and people are far apart—people of honor are dead as the lies, actors, phonies and clowns call themselves life and walk around dead without souls and raise their kids to be just like them
>
> Two sides—in and out—two wheels—US Army, German Army. I was in truth on, in and around the two of them—into one wheel, in three points—three wheels = one.
>
> What is in and out has been set in minds-brains thought patterns by the pure discontent of the minds-brains of people who want to get away from themselves—run away from being in where they are a—running to escape themselves in books, TVs, movies, money—always thinking there is a Somewhere Else.
>
> I've watched it all my life—men who can't stand themselves and be locked in a room alone is hell to their minds. Their heads are programmed so hard to mothers [sic] discontent they got to keep running.
>
> Here is everywhere in the English word of Manson that is true in NOW as of 1934 and World War One—of Charles Maddox of Kentucky Nancy Maddox Queen of King James. You can only find God inside your own space and love, and if you can't be at peace within yourself no amount of money or anything will ever work. Drugs—roots and herbs—do help some but the final and last breakdown is inside you and that is Out. You are your own in and your own out. Peace and love and good is [sic] Now, Forever, Always and Nothing.

(These writings were obtained in 2007 from Charles Manson's Internet site: http://www.mansondirect.com.) This is typical of the way Charlie expressed himself to me that afternoon. I could understand the fascination that impressionable young girls had with the complexity of his disturbed mind, especially considering that the "Family" members were high on drugs. I spent almost an hour listening to Charlie's raving. Other than having a unique experience, I decided that meeting Charlie was a waste of time and probably was a mistake. My curiosity was satisfied but what was the real point of the meeting? Charlie's Counselor appeared and escorted me out of the security wing. He asked *What did you think of Charlie?* Collecting my thoughts I replied *I think Charlie is very ill—mentally ill. And I believe he should be transferred to Vacaville where he can receive treatment for mental illness.* I was still a newcomer. What could I possibly know about appropriate treatment for Charles Manson? I was amazed to read in the newspaper two days later that Charles Manson had been transferred to the prison at Vacaville. In May, 2007 at age 72, Charles Manson skipped his parole hearing. He then was denied parole for five more years.

Warnings of Trouble

In November there was a growing undercurrent of angry, dissatisfied residents because of restrictions on parties. Residents' morale was deteriorating. The staff members picked up whisperings and rumors that there would be a riot. A group of residents had organized themselves into a "Prisoners Union" unbelievably! I wondered what else could go wrong. Would we have a sit-down strike or a refusal to work? Would we have to negotiate with residents? We assumed that a "riot" meant residents would march into the campus, sit down and refuse to go to work. None of us imagined a demonstration where residents would try to trash and burn the prison.

You've never heard of a riot at a women's prison, because everyone knows women do not riot. Walt Cooper told me *Women will never do that. Men riot, women don't riot in prison.* It seems the thinking was that when men riot, they kill each other, hold Correctional Officers as hostages, make demands and damage the facility. It could have been like that at CIW, but I believed our residents did not have the appetite for such behavior. Men turn into a mob behind a leader while women are less inclined to surge behind a figurehead with intent to inflict injuries and cause property destruction. That was our thinking in November, 1975.

Residents' frustrations came to a head with an actual riot, just at the start of the Christmas Season. The incident that triggered it was the residents' expectations regarding rules governing the holiday parties. I felt these parties were appropriate at Christmas and was happy about holding these in the spirit of the Season. Each cottage group along with its Counselor was planning its own party. To the residents this meant they would decorate their own cottage and their families would come into the cottages with gifts and baskets of home-made food. As the Counselors worked on planning the parties, I began to hear rumblings of staff members dissatisfaction that the parties on this scale would become unmanageable. There was a mounting problem with the Correctional Officers because all the plans included hundreds of visitors coming inside CIW. It involved the Correctional Officers and the Counselors <u>volunteering</u> their free time on Saturdays and Sundays to supervise hundreds of visitors carrying goods and gifts that had to be carefully screened. A group of Counselors got together and said they had changed their minds; they did not want to supervise the parties. That was the beginning of a bad situation. I felt anxious that the tenuous activities keeping CIW calm were about to be disturbed. So after my coaxing, they reluctantly agreed to proceed with the plans.

The first two parties were held on a Saturday with a blustery Santa Ana wind chilling everyone's bones. Families began arriving outside the main gate with their crying babies, Christmas gifts and food baskets. It took several hours for the Correctional Officers and Counselors to search the visitors and their goods and admit them through the gate. During this delay the visitors stood outside feeling cold and hostile. Meantime the residents inside were angry that it was taking so long to search their families and visitors. Residents and visitors became abusive to the Correctional Officers and the Counselors who were doing the searching. Instead of appreciating everybody's volunteering to facilitate these events, the residents of the two cottages having parties were dissatisfied and uncooperative. Finally, the hundreds of visitors were passed through the gate and the parties began.

When these visitors came in, we stamped their hands with ultraviolet ink. This was to differentiate a visitor from a resident who might be trying to blend into the line of visitors exiting the prison. When the parties finally ended about 6:00 P.M. the visitors were ushered out of the prison. It was time for residents to go into their rooms to be counted. When we discovered that two residents were missing, I ordered an immediate lock-down and had the Chino police put out an All Points Bulletin (APB) while initiating a campus-wide search. A "snitch" told us the missing residents had put on wigs. One of them picked up a baby and they both walked out the gate with the visitors. The staff members had failed to be vigilant in checking the stamped hands. The residents had disguised themselves so they weren't recognized by the staff and now were at large.

About 9:00 P.M. several Correctional Officers and the eight Correctional Counselors walked into my office. Sharon, one of the most forthright of the Counselors spoke for the group. She declared *We're not going to take responsibility for any more parties. We're not staffed to handle hundreds of visitors. We're not being paid to do that. Why should we do this when we could be home with our families? We froze our asses today and we're not going to do it again.* This negative attitude by staff worried me. I replied that they were wasting their time with protests because as of this date further parties such as these are canceled. I asked them what they were doing to get the population settled down and to prevent future escapes. The Counselors had not thought through these challenges and fell silent. I sent them scurrying to gather the information and do damage control. Meantime, the Resident Council members were told that the subsequent parties that had been planned to be held in the cottages were cancelled. Instead, these parties would be held in the Residents' Visiting Room with their families. That triggered the great eruption of anger by the residents against the administration and the staff.

The Riot

Several days before Christmas around 7:00 P.M., the big trouble began. The new family visiting rules that allowed parties only in the Residents' Visiting Room had lighted the fuse. A group of residents grabbed the large, decorated Christmas tree from the center of the campus and threw it through the glass picture window into my office. Then they set the office on fire. Disturbances erupted all over the campus as residents came running out of the cottages. They picked up stones and broke the windows of the cottages, threw furniture through the windows and began trashing the entire facility. They stole items out of each other's rooms and threw television sets around. They rushed to the Village Cafeteria, broke in and threw around food, the pots and pans and the dishes. They broke into the schoolroom, the library and most of the buildings ringing the campus. They marched on the Hospital and tried to break into the pharmacy to get at the drugs.

By that time the staff pulled together and sounded the alarm. Captain Madge phoned me at home that the residents had taken over the Administration Building. From that area they could just walk out the glass front door to freedom. Apparently they climbed into my office through the broken window on the campus side, then through my office, and ran down the hall toward the lobby. The staff members were taken by surprise and had regrouped in the lobby. They weren't armed and there wasn't anything to prevent escapes. The residents had not expected to make such progress so luckily, they did not press their good fortune. At that moment all of them who had come that far could have escaped. There was absolutely no security and the residents did not realize that we were so ill prepared. Accordingly, they fell back and were herded by Correctional Officers back into my office behind a locked door.

I was worried and apprehensive as I arrived on the scene, thanks to Bill's skillful driving. Bill told me he was going to stick around. Of course he was! I could not imagine him driving off saying *I'll be at home; call me when you need to be picked up.*

A conjugal visit was going on in the Family Visiting Unit upstairs so that family had to be locked into the Visiting Unit to keep them all safe. But then the resident called down and said she needed milk for her baby. Imagine! We did find milk for her in the middle of this crisis.

The TV stations' reporters and cameramen arrived. My parents in Michigan told me that suddenly a news flash came on and there was their daughter in the middle of a prison riot being interviewed on camera. I tried to show a brave face. The riot was being covered by the major national TV networks. A riot in a women's prison is really NEWS! I knew I had lost control of the situation and that the buck stopped here. I didn't have time to worry about my job security; I was worried about what the final outcome would be. Would the staff and residents be unharmed? Would we regain control in a reasonable time and manner? What would be the outcome? I was afraid that my lack of experience would adversely affect the final results.

The State Police sent several squad cars and a helicopter. Residents told me later they thought there were armed Correctional Officers in the helicopters and that helped to control everything. The residents thought they were going to be shot. Many of the residents wanted to cooperate and just get the disturbance over with, as they were not participating.

The CIW Fire Chief and his crew eased our antique fire truck into the center of the campus, where it promptly broke down. The residents stoned the firefighters and cut holes in the water hoses. Fires were suppressed by the Chino and Corona Fire Departments who arrived on the scene. The scene was violent because residents were throwing all sorts of objects, but it appeared they weren't trying to kill anyone. By the time I arrived at the prison the CIW armory had been opened and shotguns and tear gas were being issued. There was no ammunition to be found! The campus looked like war had been declared. I wasn't sure what to do, having never commanded a war. Luckily, Bill not only stuck around, he seemed to have placed himself in the thick of things. He had trained and commanded Special Forces troops and was experienced in riot control.

The Watch Officer was in the Control Room, down the hall from my office. He was getting frantic telephone calls from staff members who were trapped in cottages and surrounded by residents. He got a call saying a staff member was trapped in the Maintenance Shop and the residents were about to break in to get the hammers, saws and other potential weapons. A scream from another staff member came over the telephone to let us know that residents were trying to break into the pharmacy to get drugs.

At that point, Bill felt he could no longer stand around just giving me moral support. He picked up an unloaded shotgun from the counter and addressed some female Correctional Officers who were standing in the lobby. *Follow me* he ordered and four of them grabbed unloaded shotguns and followed him into the darkness of the melee. I was relieved that Bill was taking charge of calming the situation and regaining control. I ordered that no one was to fire a weapon without Bill's permission. I did not realize that the shotguns were not loaded.

Bill told me later that he did have second thoughts about leading a small group of hesitant female Correctional Officers into the rioting. However, his military training with riot control dictated that someone had to take charge, particularly when the administrative area of the prison stood a chance to be overrun. He believed I was depending on him to help quell the disturbance. Once in the yard, the mission was to identify the principal trouble makers and neutralize them. The advance through the yard wasn't a cakewalk. In the single story cottages, some residents who had broken the windows were playing Frisbee® with the glass fragments. Past this gauntlet, it was fairly straightforward to identify the real trouble makers who were on the campus urging unwilling residents to "get in on the action, sisters!"

The staff refused to let me leave the Administration Building to go onto the campus. Leaning through the broken window in my office, the Watch Commander fired a pistol into the air to get the attention of the residents. Over the campus loudspeaker I announced, *Go back to your rooms and you won't get hurt.* Most of the residents tried to do that, but by then, many of the cottages had fires inside and were too smoky. There was no place to go for the residents that wanted to stay out of trouble. I then announced *If you can't go into your cottage, go to the middle of the campus and sit on the ground with your hands on your head!* About ninety percent of them huddled there in the middle of the campus, in a state of absolute fright. Imagine the scene, the lights broken, flying sheets of glass hurled through the air, shadowy figures running wild, fires blazing and residents screaming. Bill and his small patrol were searching the vast flaming campus and had succeeded in identifying and isolating many of the core trouble makers. I started to feel more confident and relieved that the damage wasn't worse and that staff and residents were not injured.

During the chaos, Nancy Graham, the audio-visual teacher, ran around in the midst of the confusion trying to find a certain resident who was in her class. Nancy wanted to obtain the resident's term paper so Nancy could grant her college credit. When I encountered a breathless Nancy pausing in the Administration Building she sheepishly admitted she was trying to keep her college credit program from being cancelled.

The Watch Commander resumed his place in the Command Center and we put our heads together to come up with a plan to regain order. The staff members on the campus with walkie-talkies kept us informed. When the fires were mostly contained, Bill and his small band of Correctional Officers herded the group of trouble makers to a place on the campus grounds away from the rest of the residents. At this point, official reinforcements from other prisons and agencies arrived on the campus. Bill was content to withdraw quietly with no acknowledgment, but it was not to be that easy. Someone in the reinforcement group snitched on him to the Department. I soon would receive an official letter from the Corrections Department requesting the facts concerning his presence with a weapon on the campus during the riot.

Roland Wood, Warden from the nearby California Rehabilitation Center in Corona, and Bert Griggs, Warden of California Institution for Men (CIM) arrived with some of their Correctional Officers to lend support. During all this, there were many residents trying to help the staff members while other residents were continuing to trash and burn the place. I don't think the rioters were deliberately trying to hurt anyone. It was vandalism out of control and they were venting their frustrations by trashing the prison.

While no one was seriously hurt, some did get minor cuts and bruises. Several residents rallied around and brought gurneys to carry the slightly wounded to the hospital. The doctors reported for duty, and ambulances were standing by. After two hours, we regained complete control of the prison. Our headcounts indicated all residents accounted for. That was a huge relief to me. What if dozens had escaped? I refused to think about that. The immediate task was administering to the residents, seeing if everyone was all right and having the doctors administer tranquilizers to those who needed them. Many of the residents were hysterical and frightened.

In Sacramento, Director Enomoto gathered his top staff and placed a call to me. I was on the speaker phone giving play-by-play accounts concerning the status and welfare of the residents and our clean-up operations. Around 9:00 P.M., key staff members gathered to prepare their reports, a task that lasted almost all night. The "top brass" kept saying *This is fantastic; this is the first time we've ever had a disturbance without anyone being seriously hurt or shot.* They could not get over the relatively satisfactory outcome of this incident. They were reassured by the decisions I made. I wasn't asking them what to do I was telling them what we would do.

When the trouble started, the residents had focused on demonstrating. By the time they thought about going over the fence, the perimeter was ringed with police and other back-up people. We did a good job handling the situation. No one escaped and fewer were hurt than anyone could have imagined. It didn't take long for the residents to realize they had totally disrupted their living areas, classes and work programs.

The riot happened the week before Christmas. Residents were locked-down in secure areas until the cottages could be repaired. Although the cement buildings did not burn, the curtains, day-room furniture, pianos, almost everything burnable was lost. Residents could not come out of their rooms into the lounges and day rooms or showers because all the windows were broken. The Wardens from neighboring prisons offered their facilities and anything we needed. They loaned extra staff for the next few weeks to help clean up and relieve CIW staff members who were working around the clock.

Staff members were trying to get the broken glass removed and get the facility operational so it could be re-opened. That seemed to take forever. The most vexing problem was establishing an adequate temporary food service. Remember, residents operated the kitchen. So with no cooks or helpers, preparing and serving food was difficult. Staff members managed to provide brown-bag meals but nothing was particularly appealing.

I told the Correctional Counselors to meet with the residents to get a sense of their attitudes and intended behavior. Based on their reports we gradually began moving toward normal operations. In Sacramento the "top brass" was getting nervous because CIW still was locked-down.

Bill and I bought a good sized Christmas tree and ornaments. It was placed in the Visiting Room and several trusted residents were released to decorate it. Two days before Christmas we announced that CIW would not be going back to full-scale activity just yet, but visitors would be permitted for Christmas. Residents had to stay in their rooms or their cottages or around the exercise area. They were not allowed to wander around on campus or go to their jobs. Residents could make phone calls to their families. A few of the kitchen workers and cooks were released so an improved feeding system could occur. Nothing was quite back to normal, but by Christmas Day, the lock-down had ended. I felt relieved. We had come through a very rough time and had triumphed. I appreciated the cooperation of the staff members, all of whom behaved exceptionally. I couldn't begin to tell Bill the depth of my love and appreciation for him in bringing security back to CIW and to me.

The Corrections Department gave CIW a special $600,000 cash infusion to cover costs of rebuilding the damaged facilities and paying for the overtime that had accrued. This special funding was certainly needed but, in retrospect, if we had adequate overtime funds in our regular operating budget, the riot might never have happened.

The Counselors interviewed the residents who had been on the campus during the riot to have them identify participants. By the time all the reports had been written about who had done what to whom, we had a plan. The Psychiatric Treatment Unit (PTU) was the most secure place at CIW. It could house about sixty residents. It was isolated inside a secure chain link fence and had its own classroom, kitchen, visiting room and exercise yard. It was completely self-contained. PTU would be a perfect place to isolate the trouble makers. I took a risk and moved all of the psychiatric patients into one of the campus cottages and prepared PTU for its new function. After we established who was going to be placed in PTU we started making arrangements for support staff members and programs to be brought there.

Meantime, on campus the buildings were cleaned and windows replaced. We were working to get the rest of the campus back to normal and resuming classes and programs. I spent about eight hours a day holding individual hearings with about sixty of the identified trouble makers. A panel of five of us would talk to a resident for several hours about her case, her total behavior, her actions during the riot, why she was in prison. The number of documented violations in her folder and her general attitude told us a great deal about her. At the end of these evaluation sessions about twenty residents were released to go back to the general population and the remaining forty were directed to live in PTU. I assigned our best Correctional Counselors, best teachers, best cooks and best services to PTU. I believed that enrichment would bring faster results. We started vocational training programs and schooling there. The isolation of PTU from the rest of the campus broke up some lesbian partnerships and there was screaming through the fence. These residents were angry about being locked-up in PTU and wrote to their congressional members and senators to protest.

Walt Cooper, my boss, flew down to CIW to tell me *The Department doesn't like the lockup unit at CIW. Nobody buys the idea that women are dangerous. This is bad PR, and it doesn't look good.* I said *There are lockup units in every men's prison in the State and the hard-core prisons are total lockup prisons. You have Folsom, you have San Quentin but CIW has nothing like that. We have dangerous trouble makers who keep the whole prison in an uproar. We must have a lockup so we can regain and maintain control of this place.* Nothing was getting resolved through our discussion so Cooper flew back to Sacramento. I was worried that I had alienated my boss. What should I have done differently? I worried about my job security. I had done my best, and it wasn't good enough. It helped that I believed I was a "whole" person and therefore could make mistakes.

The twenty residents who were released were moved into one of the cottage wings with double staffing of the best Correctional Officers assigned to that cottage. Doubling up on custody staff there meant not having staff elsewhere where they were needed. To accommodate this shortage of personnel, an "honor" cottage was established without Correctional Officers being present around the clock.

After CIW settled down and the reconstruction/rehabilitation plan was in place, the Corrections Department sent me a letter demanding to know why William Carey was on the campus in the middle of the conflict. Bill thought briefly about the ramifications of the letter, knowing it could lead to serious consequences for me. He formed what he believed to be a bullet-proof explanation. The spin was that CIW was boarding several federal prisoners due to overcrowding at the federal prison in San Diego. Bill is a retired regular Army officer and in that capacity he is forever an officer of the United States, by Act of Congress. The federal prisoners boarded at CIW were potentially in harm's way during the riot. Bill, being the only federal officer on the scene, decided it was his duty to become involved. This rebuttal was sent to the Corrections Department and within a few days came a terse written response that said in effect, all right, but do not let it happen again! *Not to worry* quoting Bill.

Investigation and Resignation

The last week of January, 1976, the Department of Corrections assigned an African American attorney named Mary Slater, to investigate why CIW had established a lockup unit. No one considered that all of the California men's prisons had used lockup units for years. It was only the women's prison that never had been allowed to use a full time lockup unit. Mary Slater appeared in my office one afternoon with a specific mission. She spoke firmly saying *Mrs. Carey, I understand that you have a lockup unit here. I would like to inspect that unit now.* I was proud to show it to her. I pointed out that the best Counselors and teachers and food service personnel were in the PTU. I toured her through the unit and encouraged her to talk with the residents there.

Ace and Lucy were there, and many others of our well-known residents. They smiled and called out greetings. A number of residents were pleased to see me there and came over to hug me, much to Mary's surprise. A few residents complained to Mary that they weren't being fairly treated and they weren't permitted to socialize with the residents on campus. There were about four of them who wanted to be back with their lesbian partners. In a women's prison the sexual play between the residents often becomes an intense lesbian relationship. They are not "gay" in the sense of being homosexual, and when they are paroled, most of them return happily to their husbands or boyfriends as if it never happened.

At the end of Mary's tour Bill arrived and together we drove Mary to the Chino airport. As we waited for her plane to arrive, she was strangely silent. Then, facing me, she asked *Mrs. Carey, what is the ethnic balance of the women in the lockup unit? Is it 33% Caucasian, 33% African American and 33% Hispanic?* I replied *Mary, that's not how it is!* I was astonished. Mary quickly retorted *Mrs. Carey that is just how it is. You must be a racist. I know you're a racist. Let me tell you, if you do not have an ethnic balance of women in that lockup unit by tomorrow morning, you are going to release all of those women into the general population immediately.* I had worked diligently to achieve the goals of the Corrections Department's Affirmative Action goals. The residents in the PTU lockup virtually had selected themselves in terms of their behavior during the riot, and the panel who decided which residents would be assigned there was ethnically balanced. There were more African Americans and Hispanics than Caucasians on the Hearings panel but that did not make any difference to Mary. I had tried to be straight-forward and neutral about the Hearings. I am the last person to be called a racist!

Her demand was outrageous. There was no way I would release trouble makers into the general population in exchange for randomly-selected residents from the campus in order to achieve an ethnic balance. I knew we had been extremely fair in selecting residents for intense rehabilitation and attention. Mary's demand was the culmination of the bureaucratic nonsense I had been fighting for almost a year. Anger welled up in me, making it hard to speak. I said *Well, let me tell you, Mary, this is what you are going to have by tomorrow morning. My resignation!* I turned away to hide my rage. Without any acknowledgement or retort, Mary hurried to her plane and flew off to Sacramento.

After Bill and I arrived home, the full impact of the situation came to me. Bill and I discussed these unfolding events into the late hours of the night. While I was disturbed and upset about Mary's visit, I was surprised to feel relieved that I soon would be free to resume my normal life. I would be able to continue my consulting business without too many obstacles, as the greater Los Angeles area offered unlimited business opportunities. Bill had established himself and was a consultant to several clients in the automotive after-market sales business. With this income and his military retirement, we could remain afloat comfortably until I became established. The real issue at hand however was developing my game plan with the Corrections Department after I had defied their "messenger lady." I felt anxiety, along with my relief.

The next morning was January 31. I phoned Walt Cooper to report Mary's visit and her unconditional demand. Cooper knew all about Mary's visit. He told me that he, Jerry Enomoto, Harold Williams and the Department's Public Relations man, Phil Guthrie, were flying down to Chino on the late afternoon plane. This would be my opportunity, so I typed my letter of resignation and met them that evening at the Pine Tree Motel. Before they could speak, I said *Gentlemen, I would like you to accept my resignation effective immediately. You know why. The last straw was when Mary Slater came to CIW and accused me of being a racist because there was not an ethnic balance of residents in the lockup unit. She ordered me to release all the residents in lockup unless I was willing to create an ethnic balance there. You know, this is an outrageous demand. To make an artificial balance! No thank you! Find someone else to be the fall guy! I'll meet you at CIW in the morning and turn over the keys. Good night!* Driving home, I felt liberated.

The next morning the "top brass" had preceded me and was waiting in my office. I said to Beverly *Please assemble the staff in the conference room in ten minutes.* The staff assembled quickly, no one saying a word. I was in command, probably more than I've ever been. I said to the "top brass" *Gentlemen, if you will remain here in my office I'll be with you shortly.*

I walked into the conference room and stood at the head of the long table. The room was eerily quiet as I made my announcement. *Effective immediately, I have resigned. I am sure Walt Cooper will appoint an interim Superintendent quickly but meanwhile Walt Cooper will be your boss until I'm replaced. If you have any questions refer these to him. Thank you all for the cooperation and support you've given me. It has been my pleasure to work with you.* I had a lump in my throat but managed to speak without a quaver. Beverly began to cry so hard she was inconsolable so I gently suggested that she take the rest of the day off, and sent her home with a hug. I returned to my office and asked for a letter of reference. Director Enomoto said he would be pleased to send me a letter. I replied *Thank you, Jerry, but I would like my letter now, please, before I leave. I'll wait.*

While I was waiting for my letter I walked to the PTU to say goodbye to the residents and to give them my best wishes. I went around the group, shook hands with the residents and said goodbye. As I walked out of PTU feeling frustrated and angry, I had tears in my eyes thinking of all the things I had been trying to accomplish. As I returned to the Administration Building, I thought I can't be crying now. But I was—tears were spilling down my cheeks. Marguerite, one of my favorite residents came up to me. *I hear you are leaving,* she said looking closely at me. She saw tears running down my face and she put her arms around me. *Oh, Mrs. Carey, you did the best you could, we think you're wonderful, don't cry. We're really sorry you're leaving us.* Marguerite's false eyelashes were almost an inch long, and as she also began to cry, they floated down her cheeks riding on her tears. I gave her a hug and a faint smile and walked on through the Administration Building into my office.

I phoned Bill asking him to pick me up at CIW and waited in my office, gazing out the window at residents going about their business. Director Enomoto had indeed dictated the letter of reference. When the letter was typed and signed, Phil Guthrie brought it to me. This is what it said.

February 3, 1976
TO WHOM IT MAY CONCERN:

Brook Carey served for nearly one year as Superintendent of the California Institution for Women, one of the most demanding and difficult administrative posts in the California Department of Corrections.

The California Institution for Women is the state's only correctional institution for female offenders.

As Superintendent, Mrs. Carey was in charge of a Staff of 330 employees and administered an annual budget of approximately $7,000,000. The prison houses about 750 prisoners. It includes a wide ranging program including medical services, vocational training, academic education, prison industry, counseling services and basic security activities.

During the time she was Superintendent, Mrs. Carey instituted several long needed changes in a traditional operational pattern. She demonstrated considerable management skill in confronting varied administrative challenges.

While she was in the post she also displayed admirable calm and poise in an extreme emergency during the course of a serious inmate disturbance.

Mrs. Carey is, in my opinion, a highly talented administrator with a wealth of management skills.

I would be pleased to provide additional comments regarding Mrs. Carey as they might be desired.

(Signed) J. J. Enomoto
Director of Corrections

After I read the letter, Phil walked toward me. Facing me and putting his hands on my shoulders, he looked into my eyes and very slowly with emphasis on each word said *You ... are ... a very classy ... lady!* I replied *Thank you, Phil. Here are my keys.* I smiled as I handed him the large ring of keys. *Don't forget to lock up!* After a swift handshake, I walked rapidly down the long hall and through the door that buzzed into the lobby. I felt numb. Bill's car was parked in front, engine running. I jumped in quickly. As we pulled away, glancing back, I saw some residents lined up inside the chain link fence, crying and sadly waving goodbye. I lowered my window and waved back. We drove quickly away down winding roads through the cow pastures. That was the last time I saw CIW. The accidental Warden was history.

In Retrospect

The letter from Sue, our Athletic Director, February 5, 1976

Dear Brook,

You have been very much in my thoughts these past few days so I decided to write and let you know what's on my mind and in my heart.

Unfortunately you came to CIW at a very bad time. Morale was low, both among staff and inmates and the whole place suffered from an inconsistency in policy and planning. There was much that needed to be done but because you weren't from within the Department many looked upon you as an outsider. The acceptance and support that is so necessary for the success of any job just wasn't there. It was an impossible and regrettable situation.

And yet, despite all the obstacles, you made a constant effort to do the job and to do it well. I was always impressed by your positive approach to things and the poise with which you were able to function under very trying circumstances. You brought much to your work and there are many who benefited from your time here.

So what I really want to say is thank you for all that you are and all that you did. I hope the future holds many good things for you.

I send my love and gratitude, Brook, and a promise that you will always have a place in my prayers. I feel enriched for having known you.

Sue

Sue's letter made me cry. She had captured all the challenge and difficulty I faced and had given me the pat on the back I had missed. Before working at CIW, I never felt blocked from things I wanted to do, and so I thought it must be my lack of experience in the Criminal Justice System that made me feel out of step with the Corrections Department. I set about reading and studying, trying to train myself. One month into my service, I had emergency surgery that required three weeks recuperation at home. To use my time wisely, we obtained a copy of the California Penal Code that I read from first page to last. It was frustrating to be recuperating at home when my head and heart were focused upon my new job and I felt guilty for not being there.

What was said about me after I resigned? That I was an experiment, ahead of my own time, that I was about three years ahead of where I should have been. No one warned me that I was an experiment, and this is the up-side and this is the down-side, and it might work if you do such-and-such. I had virtually zero input from Walt Cooper, my boss. I think the job would not have been impossible if I had more help or support. AllenBrown and Ron Burke were rivals of each other, usually on opposite ends of an argument. When I would go to the Deputy Superintendents for advice, I seldom heard the same advice from the two of them, so I did not know who or what to believe.

In previous positions, I took actions that made sense in a corporate boardroom; these types of actions were out of place at CIW. It almost appeared to be a male collusion. The system at CIW was set up so that the Superintendent was virtually powerless, and the men were running the prison. I only learned later that my two male Deputy Superintendents had the pipeline to my male bosses at the Corrections Department. I honestly believed that Corrections was an inflexible system, everyone else was making it in that system so **the problem must lie with me. I did not understand that many problems were inherent in the system.**

February 3, 1976, the Corrections Department appointed a woman as Superintendent of CIW who previously was a Deputy Superintendent there before I arrived. When I was appointed, that woman was angry about being passed over for promotion so the Department had reassigned her to Soledad prison. She and two subsequent Superintendents were terminated after short terms in my vacated position.

In April, 1980, Director Jiro "Jerry" Enomoto was transferred out of the Department of Corrections into another position with the State. Enomoto, at first refused to leave and filed a law suit to keep his job. Within two weeks, he dropped the law suit and he was gone. Ruth Russian, an experienced manager, was appointed to replace Enomoto. She immediately terminated three Wardens and Harold Williams and several others of the top executive staff from the Corrections Department. It was alleged that the terminations were because the prison system was in a major crisis and new management at the top was the only solution.

When I learned of the executive management terminations at the Corrections Department, I confess I felt vindicated. It appears that my thinking I was "out of step" with the management perhaps was confirmation that the incompetent managers may not have been ME! When the "top brass" was terminated, it became more apparent that none of the Department executives had "business" experience and that certainly would contribute to the problems in the Corrections system.

Two subsequent Directors resigned after short terms on the job. The severe problems in the California prisons continued unabated. From the April 25, 1983 *Los Angeles Times*, "No one wants to sign on as the cruise director of the Titanic" said Jeff Thompson, executive director of the California Correctional Peace Officers Association that represents 8,500 prison guards. California has built three new women's prisons. The challenges I faced undoubtedly have been diminished because of that. I have great respect for the people who work in California's prisons.

I felt angry and discouraged when I left and did not want to let anyone know that. I was dealing with what I perceived as a major failure on my part. However, the experience I gained at CIW helped me grow personally and I became more empathetic with subordinates and more confident in my creative problem solving abilities. So the experience wasn't a complete failure, after all.

When I left, I was emotionally drained; I hadn't slept in days because I was on call after the riot twenty-four hours a day. For the first few years, I just wanted to forget about CIW. I did not think about it for a long time. Until now.

Epilogue

It was time to go back to work. I was recruited to be Vice President of Administration with the Corporate Headquarters of Century 21 Real Estate Corporation in Irvine, California. It was challenging and I had no time to think back upon my year at CIW. Century 21 grew from 300 offices to 10,000 offices while I worked there.

After three years, I left Century 21 and enrolled in a Master of Science program (Organizational Development) at Pepperdine University. There were twenty-seven people in the class; three of us graduated on time. I am proud of that achievement. I then established a franchise development corporation in California and designed and implemented dozens of franchise systems for clients.

In 1978, Bill was hired by the Pacific Region of Volkswagen of America as a Sales Trainer. Within a few years he received an extraordinary six-level promotion to be National Manager of Dealer Relations for Volkswagen, Porsche and Audi, stationed in Detroit. The cartwheel effect was working perfectly as it then was my turn to follow him back to Detroit where I continued my business consulting and franchise development business in Michigan with dozens of client companies.

In 1987, upon Bill's request we were moved by Volkswagen from Michigan to Phoenix, Arizona where he retired a year later from the automotive world and I recruited him to work in my consulting businesses. We relocated to San Antonio, Texas in July, 2005 and now are happily working and enjoying our lives there together.

978-0-595-71967-9
0-595-71967-8